Drama Techniques in Language Learning

CAMBRIDGE HANDBOOKS FOR LANGUAGE TEACHERS

This is a series of practical guides for teachers of English and other languages. Illustrative examples are usually drawn from the field of English as a foreign or second language, but the ideas and techniques described can equally well be used in the teaching of any language.

In this series:

Drama Techniques in Language Learning – A resource book of communication activites for language teachers
by Alan Maley and Alan Duff

Games for Language Learning
by Andrew Wright, David Betteridge and Michael Buckby

Discussions that Work – Task-centred fluency practice *by Penny Ur*

Once Upon a Time – Using stories in the language classroom
by John Morgan and Mario Rinvolucri

Teaching Listening Comprehension *by Penny Ur*

Keep Talking – Communicative fluency activities for language teaching
by Friederike Klippel

Working with Words – A guide to teaching and learning vocabulary
by Ruth Gairns and Stuart Redman

Learner English – A teacher's guide to interference and other problems
edited by Michael Swan and Bernard Smith

Testing Spoken Language – A handbook of oral testing techniques
by Nic Underhill

Literature in the Language Classroom – A resource book of ideas and activities
by Joanne Collie and Stephen Slater

Dictation – New methods, new possibilities
by Paul Davis and Mario Rinvolucri

Grammar Practice Activities – A practical guide for teachers
by Penny Ur

Testing for Language Teachers *by Arthur Hughes*

Pictures for Language Learning *by Andrew Wright*

Five-Minute Activities – A resource book of short activities
by Penny Ur and Andrew Wright

The Standby Book – Activities for the language classroom
edited by Seth Lindstromberg

Lessons from Nothing – Activities for language teachers with limited time and resources *by Bruce Marsland*

Beginning to Write – Writing activities for elementary and intermediate learners
by Arthur Brookes and Peter Grundy

Ways of Doing – Students explore their everyday and classroom processes
by Paul Davis, Barbara Garside and Mario Rinvolucri

Using Newspapers in the Classroom
by Paul Sanderson

Drama Techniques in Language Learning

A resource book of
communication activities
for language teachers

Alan Maley and Alan Duff

CAMBRIDGE
UNIVERSITY PRESS

PUBLISHED BY THE PRESS SYNDICATE OF THE UNIVERSITY OF CAMBRIDGE
The Pitt Building, Trumpington Street, Cambridge, United Kingdom

CAMBRIDGE UNIVERSITY PRESS
The Edinburgh Building, Cambridge CB2 2RU, UK
40 West 20th Street, New York, NY 10011–4211, USA
10 Stamford Road, Oakleigh, VIC 3166, Australia
Ruiz de Alarcón 13, 28014 Madrid, Spain
Dock House, The Waterfront, Cape Town 8001, South Africa

http://www.cambridge.org

First published 1978
Fourth printing 1980
Second edition 1982
Nineteenth printing 2001

Printed in the United Kingdom at the University Press, Cambridge

Library of Congress catalogue card number: 82-1191

British Library Cataloguing in Publication data
Maley, Alan

Drama techniques in language learning. – 2nd ed.
(Cambridge handbooks for language teachers)
1. Languages modern – Study and teaching
2. Drama in education
I. Title   II. Duff, Alan
418.'007   PB36

ISBN 0 521 24907 4 hardback
ISBN 0 521 28868 1 paperback

Contents

Acknowledgements

We are grateful for the inspiration, encouragement and advice of the following: John Allen, Martin Banham, Philip Berry, Patrick Early, John Hodgson, Michael Patterson, Elayne Phillips.

The authors and publishers are grateful to the authors, publishers and others who have given their permission for the use of copyright material identified in the text. It has not been possible to identify sources of all the material used and in such cases the publishers would welcome information from copyright holders.

Rank Xerox (UK) Ltd for the advertisements on p. 97; Routledge & Kegan Paul Ltd (UK) and E.P. Dutton, Inc. (US) for extracts from *The Book of Heroic Failures* by Stephen Pile on pp. 111–12 © 1979 by Stephen Pile; John Walmsley for the photographs on p. 116; *Newsweek* for the extract from 'New Products and Processes: Medical Maneuvers' on p. 155; *The Sunday Times* for the extract from 'Hard day at the cassette, darling?' by Robert Whyment on pp. 155–6; *The Times* for the illustration on p. 156; Faber and Faber Ltd (UK) and Random House Inc. (US) for the poem 'If I could tell you' by W.H. Auden on pp. 184–5; Christiane Charillon for the cartoons by Sempé on pp. 193–4; Victor Gollancz Ltd for the extract from *The Only Revolution* by J. Krishnamurti on p. 204; Weidenfeld and Nicolson Ltd for extracts from *The Eye and the Brain* by Richard Gregory on pp. 204–5; Chatto and Windus Ltd (UK) and Simon and Schuster Inc.(US) for the extract from *Mortal Licence* by Richard Selzer on pp. 204–5; Victor Gollancz Ltd for the extract from *Language, Truth and Logic* by A.J. Ayer on p. 205; Little, Brown and Co. for the extract from *The Complete Letters of Vincent Van Gogh* on p. 205; Jonathan Cape Ltd (UK) and Deborah Rogers Ltd (US) for the poem by Adrian Henri from *The Best of Henri* on p. 205; The Menard Press for poems 1–4 on pp. 208–9 from *Alphabetical and Letter Poems* ed. Peter Mayer; Secker and Warburg Ltd for the extract from 'Alphobiabet' by Stewart Brown from *The Gregory Awards 1980* ed. Porter and Sergeant on p. 209; Deborah Rogers Ltd for the poems by Adrian Henri, 'Love is' from *Penguin Modern Poets 10* and 'Me' from *The Best of Henri* (Cape) on pp. 211 and 217 © 1967 by Adrian Henri; Edinburgh University Press for the poem by Edwin Morgan from *The Second Life* on p. 213; Jonathan Cape Ltd (UK) and A.D. Peters & Co Ltd (US) for the extracts from *Darkness at Noon* by Arthur Koestler on p. 219.

The cartoon drawings are by Nigel Paige.

Fresh thoughts for a new edition

If drama were dead matter, which could be fossilized forever like an insect trapped in resin, there would be no need for this new edition of *Drama techniques in language learning*. But drama is living material, and subject to change.

What has changed?

Or, rather, what is new?

Readers familiar with the first edition of this book will find many exercises that have been retained. These are the hardy plants that have proved their resilience, and particularly their adaptability, over the past five years. Those that have been omitted have been left out not because they were *rejected* but simply to make room for 150 new ideas, all of which we felt deserved inclusion. And those ideas that have been retained are now presented with all the modifications and improvements which have been suggested by the many groups who have worked with them. In this sense, our new edition is a collective endeavour. Just as a tree in the forest produces new shoots and new branches each year, so too the ideas of the first book have grown outwards and upwards, while still drawing strength from the main stem.

Of the new ideas, many found their way naturally into the former sections on *Observation* and *Interpretation*. But there were also many which could not (or would not!) fit into the old structure. And, since drama is a living and changing material, we preferred to 'bend' the structure of the book to accommodate the new ideas, rather than 'twist' the new ideas to fit an old framework. This is why we have introduced five new sections: *Introductory exercises, Creation and invention, Word-play, Problem-solving,* and *The use of literary texts, poems and songs.* In addition, we have provided an outline of a typical *Day's Work,* to give a coherent idea of the kind of programme that might be devised using the material in this book.

The cross-reference system between sections is not meant to be watertight: the suggestions given are intended only as guidelines for possible links.

About the new sections

Introduction and warming-up

It is easy to forget, when working with a group, that each person enters the room in a different mood: some may be elated, others despondent, some tense, others relaxed, some alert, others bored. And some – just indifferent. If the group is to work together, it needs to be in harmony. The introductory exercises, simple though they may appear, are not 'games' to distract weaker students, they are *essential* activities for preparing any group to approach the more exacting tasks later to be demanded of them. They serve the same function as 'limbering up' for an athlete or 'warming up' for a football player. Their first purpose is to help all members of the group approach the later exercises in the same frame of mind – to calm the excited and to invigorate the lethargic. Their second purpose is to direct the students' thoughts and feelings towards the exercise to follow. Thus, for instance, 1.25 Feeling my space would be an excellent introduction to work on the demanding exercise 7.9 Amnesty, and 1.56 Childhood memories would be particularly suitable as a prelude to 2.13 From my album. These exercises take little time – usually no more than five minutes – but it is time well spent, for without it the group would not be in the right frame of mind to begin work.

We make no excuse for having so many introductory exercises, since they all fulfil different functions and can therefore be chosen as specifically suitable to precede one exercise rather than another. Finally, although they are described as 'introductory', there is no reason why they should not be extended into full activities if, as in the example of 1.49 Interviews, this proves desirable.

Creation and invention

This section contains many of the reformulated ideas from the earlier section on *Interpretation*. Much new material, however, has been added. Here we have introduced, for instance, the use of drawing and sketching, material or 'props' (such as, stones, corks, apples, etc.), and also music, fragments of written material (e.g. newspapers) and photographs. If there is a stress, it is on *transforming the real* into the imaginary. Many of the sketches or dramatic presentations will be close to fantasy (e.g. in designing machines that do not exist), but the language used in creating these 'fantasies' remains as 'down-to-earth' as the language required for any technical – or terrestrial – project.

Word-play

It is here that objections are most likely to be raised. Can one play with words in a foreign language? Even if one can, does it serve any purpose? Are these not exercises which favour only the linguistically talented? Where does fooling around with words get you? And so on... .

Sensitivity to language involves far more than just understanding what words mean. We must be sensitive not just to sense, but also to *sound*, and to the different ways in which the same thing may be said. Unless we have practice in *playing* with the language, we are likely to be stuck forever at a level of banality which allows for no variety of expression. The more we can experiment with different combinations of words, the better we can come to know the potential of the language we are learning. In the words of Arthur Koestler:

> Rhythm and rhyme, assonance and pun are not artificial creations, but vestigial echoes of primitive phases in the development of language, and of the even more primitive pulsations of living matter; hence our particular receptiveness for messages which arrive in a rhythmic pattern. (*The Act of Creation*)

Word-play does not mean 'being clever with the language', but rather 'exploring the language'. Once again, it must be stressed that in these exercises the product (a poem, sketch, or dramatization) is not in itself all-important; it is the language used in *developing* the idea that matters most. And this language – of discussion, proposition, acceptance, rejection, correction, etc. – remains basically the same whether one is working on an improvement to the jet engine or on the definition of an imaginary word such as 'hectoplasmolysis'.

Problem-solving

The utility of these exercises is self-evident. Not only do they develop accuracy of expression, they also give practice in *thinking* in the foreign language (sifting through information, following instructions, reducing many words to few, etc.). In addition, they have the advantage of being engrossing in themselves, as exercises. 6.1 Castles in the air is an excellent example. Here the students are not only working in English, but also *creating* something of their own. This engrossment in the task is important, because it deflects attention from the mechanical use of language, i.e. the students are basically practising 'formulae', such as : 'I suggest we...', 'Let's try it this way...', 'It would be better if...', 'Yes, but (it needs to be stable)', etc. To put it differently, the language is – paradoxically – less complex than the task!

The use of literary texts, poems and songs

In the first edition of this book we gave no more than a cold hint of what might be done with material such as we have now introduced ('Literary texts often provide good starting-points for improvisation or dramatization'). This new section is not, however, an academic afterthought designed to palliate university lecturers. It is, rather, the working-out of ideas with a practical value of which we were aware, but which we had no time to develop.

It has never been our intention to encourage parrot-like repetition or the rote learning of words in the drama exercises. This is why in this section we do not concentrate on reproducing the written word, but rather on using the text as a stimulus to fresh thought.

Inevitably, poetry proves easier to work from than prose, mainly because the context is more condensed. It would be optimistic to think that there will be no barriers to the use of poetry. Barriers there are, but they can be overcome. Let us for a moment consider the two main barriers: a) poetry is incomprehensible; b) poetry is the romantic outpouring of the soul. Both are valid descriptions – or objections. But they are no more valid than saying 'science is dry' or 'engineering is not for women'! *A poem* may be incomprehensible, or it may be a romantic outpouring of the soul, but *poetry* is not a poem. Poetry may be witty, informative, critical, impressionistic, factual (see Henry Read, 'Lessons of War'), reflective, or descriptive. A poem, suitably chosen, can often suggest more in a concentrated space than a lengthy prose text. It is with these ideas that we wish to work. The poem or song serves in much the same way as pictures do in the drama exercises – it *suggests* ideas.

If one is to work imaginatively with literature in drama activities it is necessary to overcome the preconceptions so well expressed in Roger McGough's statement: 'One must get away from poetry as something that happens where there's a glass and a bottle of water.' The purpose of these exercises is to stimulate activity which will develop in its own direction. These are drama activities, not creative-writing exercises, and the purpose is to grapple with a problem, not to produce polished prose or verse; to develop an idea, not to reproduce a text. This is by no means to suggest that the original text should be ignored, but rather that it be seen in a new context, as in 7.3 Colourful ideas or 7.9 Amnesty.

And to end with...

The ideas contained in this book are drawn from many sources. Some are our 'own', insofar as they have developed from our own practical experience. Others are adapted – ideas we have seen first used in other contexts (e.g. on radio programmes, on the stage, in business-management courses etc.) – and still others are ideas we have wittingly borrowed from other sources. Every care has been taken to acknowledge – either in the text or in the bibliography – the source of any original idea that has been incorporated in this work.

As this book may be used by different people, not only teachers, we have addressed it to an imaginary group-leader or organizer (whether or not he or she is a teacher).

The one part of the original work which remains almost unchanged is the Introduction. This is not out of laziness but simply because even now – five years later – we have no changes to make. The tree may grow new branches, but the trunk remains.

Introduction

Let us be clear from the start what we mean by 'dramatic activities'. They are activities which give the student an opportunity to use his or her own personality in creating the material on which *part* of the language class is to be based. These activities draw on the natural ability of every person to imitate, mimic and express himself or herself through gesture. They draw, too, on the student's imagination and memory, and natural capacity to bring to life parts of his or her past experience that might never otherwise emerge. They are dramatic because they arouse our interest, which they do by drawing on the unpredictable power generated when one person is brought together with others. Each student brings a different life, a different background into the class. We would like students to be able to use this when working with others.

Before going on, let us be clear what we do *not* mean by dramatic activities. We do not mean putting on plays in front of a passive audience. The stiff, self-conscious 'dramatization' of dialogues and short sketches, as occasionally produced for distraction or language reinforcement, is not what we have in mind here. Words, other people's words, which have been mechanically memorized, can turn to ashes in the speaker's mouth. They lose their savour even before they are spoken, and this we do not want.

Nor do we want students to feel that dramatic activities are part of the preparation for some great final performance. Their value is not in what they lead up to but in what they *are*, in what they bring out right *now*. So, in describing these ideas, we have no audience in mind other than the people who are *taking part*. Nobody looks on. This does not, however exclude the performance by one group for another or even by one group for all the others, if the need is felt.

Lastly, as we see them, dramatic activities are not a substitute for the psychoanalyst's couch. They are not sessions of self-liberation (complexes and hang-ups cannot be cured through them). On the other hand, they will certainly release imagination and energy – and this is hard to do in language teaching. Indeed, this is one of the purely *educational* objectives that takes us well beyond the limitations of teaching the foreign language as a subject.

About language

Most of us are familiar with the early stages of learning at least one foreign language. We may at certain times question, uneasily, the value of what we are learning; the language may seem irrelevant or artificial, the structures unwieldy, the vocabulary far-fetched. Yet we struggle on, saying 'Son chapeau est sur la chaise', 'The pupils are opening their books', or 'Mein Brüder hat es mir gesagt', in the belief that if the sentences are meaningful and correctly formed we must be learning something from them.

Much has changed in language teaching, but it is still true that the conviction that *Vocabulary + Essential Structures = Language* lies at the base of nearly every foreign language syllabus. Teaching on these lines takes account of only one aspect of the language – the intellectual aspect. But language is not purely an intellectual matter. Our minds are attached to our bodies, and our bodies to our minds. The intellect rarely functions without an element of emotion, yet it is so often just this element that is lacking in teaching material.

Many of the skills we most need when speaking a language, foreign or not, are those which are given *least* attention in the traditional text-book: adaptability (i.e. the ability to match one's speech to the person one is talking to), speed of reaction, sensitivity to tone, insight, anticipation; in short, *appropriateness*. The people we speak to during the day are not (thank goodness!) faceless citizens with conveniently pronounceable names like Brown and Grey, who rarely state anything but the obvious, and whose opinions are so bland as to give neither offence nor pleasure. The people we meet are busy, irritable, worried, flustered, tired, headachy; their breath smells, their armpits itch, food gets stuck between their teeth; they have quirks and tics and mannerisms, they speak too slowly or too fast, repeat themselves or lose the thread. They are not necessarily interesting but they are alive. And so are we. In order to talk to these people, we need to know who they are and who we are. We need to know whether the difference in our ages matters, whether we are likely to see them again, whether it is worth trying to influence them, whether they are likely to be helpful or difficult, etc. It is all very well to be able to produce statements like 'Had we not told them, they would not have come', but the words mean nothing unless we know who 'they' are and why this was said.

Drama attempts to put back some of this forgotten emotional content into language – and to put the body back too. This does not mean that we must suddenly start leaping about the room in an exaggerated fashion, but it does imply that we need to take more account of *meaning*. Much language teaching is done through structures or so-called situations in the belief that once a sentence has been correctly formulated a use can always be found for it. First comes form, then meaning. This approach can be misleading, even dangerous, because it accustoms the learner to making sentences fit into structural moulds. To use an analogy, such a learner is like an architect who designs a building before inspecting the site on which it is to be placed. There may be nothing structurally wrong with the design, but if the building is five storeys high with a stone façade, and is intended to fill the gap between two steel-and-glass skyscrapers, the architect will clearly have to put in some overtime! Practically any sentence will have an abstract meaning – a propositional or dictionary meaning – but this face value may have nothing to do with its concrete use.

Let us consider a few examples. The much maligned example that used to crop up on the first page of all language text-books, 'Is this a pen?', has now disappeared (we hope). And why? Not because it was incorrect or meaningless or useless, but because it was unnecessary and inappropriate. Try walking up to a London docker, taking a pen out of your pocket and asking him: 'Is this a pen?' If he doesn't take a swipe at you he will most likely answer, 'What the 'ell d'you take me for?' or, 'Listen, mate, if you're looking for trouble...' The question you asked was not understood as a question but as a *provocation*, which it was, for you were insulting him by suggesting he might not understand the self-evident. It is no less provoking to force the foreign language learner to go through the motions of answering inane questions simply because he or she has problems of vocabulary which the docker does not. It is not the question itself but *the reason why it was asked* that is at fault. After all, there is structurally no evident difference between 'Is this a pen?' and Macbeth's famous line, 'Is this a dagger which I see before me?' The difference lies in the feeling. Macbeth asks a question to which he knows the answer, this is true; but he asks the question because he does not want to believe what he sees. He has, then, a strong reason for speaking as he does.

Meaning, therefore, should not be confused with structure. Commands are often given in the imperative, but not always; questions are asked with question marks, but not always; continuous action in the present may be suggested by a verb ending in -*ing*, but not always. Meaning slips from one structure to another in a most elusive way. Take an innocent statement such as, 'It's eight o'clock'. This might be, variously, a substitute order ('Switch on the telly'), a concealed warning ('You'd better hurry up, they'll be here in a minute'), a form of persuasion ('Don't you think it's time we left?'), and so on. In all these examples the statement 'It's eight o'clock' takes its meaning from the intention of the speaker and his or her relation to the other person. To teach 'It's eight o'clock' as a response (and the only kind of response) to the question 'What time is it?' is to place an unnecessary restraint on the language.

Correct structures do need to be taught, nobody would deny this, but can they not be taught *meaningfully* from the very start? Consider an obvious example: the present continuous tense. This is nearly always illustrated in class by the teacher performing certain actions (opening a book, closing a window) and getting the students to reply to questions. Interest soon flags, because it seems pointless to describe what is going on in front of your eyes. Yet with a slight twist, the same actions can become interesting and the questions meaningful: all that is needed is that the observer should not know in advance why the actions are being performed. This is strikingly illustrated in two simple mime exercises : 3.17 What am I doing? and 3.18 The hotel receptionist. Drama, then, can help considerably by ensuring that language is used in an appropriate context, no matter how 'fantastic' this context may seem.

We realize, of course, that like all other activities in the classroom, drama activities cannot be 'real' simply because they are subject to the constraints the classroom imposes. Unlike more familiar activities, however, which always remain external to the student because imposed from without (and largely for the convenience of the teacher, not the student), these techniques draw upon precisely those internal resources which are essential for out-of-class use of the language.

About situation

Is it not perhaps true that the 'context' of the drama activities is simply what the text-books call 'situation' taking on a new guise? We think not. Situations, as presented in text-books, tend to take account of only one aspect of context – the physical *setting*. Once this has been established, the 'characters' are lightly sketched in and left to produce their monitored 'free dialogues'. These dialogues usually take place 'At the station', 'In the restaurant' etc. Once this setting has been fixed, the cut-out figures of Mr Brown and family are put into position. Once in position, they use two kinds of language: *situational* – words such as 'ticket', 'porter', 'timetable', which are considered indispensable when one is 'At the railway station'; *structural* – phrases which, unlike the vocabulary items, are not so much bound to the situation as enlivened by it. This is why in one book 'At the station' may serve to present the question form with WH-words ('When does the Blue Train leave?') and in another the present continuous tense ('Look, he's waving his flag!').

If one's purpose is to teach vocabulary and structure, such an approach is probably no worse than any other. But surely, then, the text-structured dialogue presentation is unnecessary? A list of words and a few correct sentences would be enough – which is exactly what most tourist phrase-books set out to provide. These books serve a specific (often useful) function: they give the rudiments of the language necessary for operating in certain surroundings. Nothing more. But most tourists have discovered to their cost that a phrase they have learnt to produce with a semblance of fluency may bring a *response* they are quite unable to follow!

How is one to right this imbalance between the great amount of material and teaching offered to students and their apparent inability to make sensible use of it? The answer is, surely, to encourage students to look at language from a different angle, to go behind the words to the actions they are most likely to perform in the language, the patterns of behaviour that lie behind all languages (*functions* such as persuading, agreeing, accepting). To do this, they need to be aware of the total situation, which is considerably richer than the mere physical setting. It will involve, at the very least, the following elements.

Setting

This is the physical environment (for example the restaurant), which may or may not directly influence the language used, as one does not talk *only* about knives, forks, and menus at a restaurant. Physical surroundings are often incidental to what is said, for example a second-hand car may be sold in a lift, a bridge designed at a birthday party. Naturally, there are occasions when physical setting prescribes language. At the dentist's it is certain that the patient's teeth will be mentioned, but what is important is not just the hole in the tooth but the nature of the person whose tooth it is. A nervous patient will need reassuring; a mistrustful patient may need convincing; an impatient patient may have to be pacified. The dentist's role, in such cases, extends far beyond the limits of the waiting-room and the reclining chair.

Role and status

As we have seen from the last example, there is an overlap between setting and role. It is most important therefore to encourage students from the start to become sensitive to the way in which our built-in views of our own roles and those of others are defined and clarified through language. Throughout the day our roles are constantly shifting. At one moment we may find ourselves in a superior position, making decisions or giving orders; at another, we may find ourselves on the receiving end, accepting decisions and carrying out commands. To return to the dentist: at one moment he might say to the nurse, 'I want you to X-ray the lower left side', and a few seconds later to the patient, 'Would you mind putting your head back a little further?' These are both commands, but the choice of language depends on the dentist's relation to patient and nurse. This role would again change if the patient were, for example, a boy of eight, to whom the dentist would most likely say, 'Come on now, put your head back. That's right.'

If we deliberately ignore the roles, we end up teaching language in a vacuum. The very fact that we open our mouths to speak implies that someone will be listening. The listener is a person. Why ignore him or her?

Mood, attitude and feeling

Even in the most formal situations, people's feelings and attitudes colour their language. For obvious reasons, this often exclamatory language is difficult to teach. Yet it is necessary from the very start to express disapproval, surprise, enthusiasm, and so on. Nothing is more difficult than to work with second-hand feelings derived from texts or dialogues, yet most students are given no more than a few innocuous exclamations ('What a pity!'...'How nice!'...) to cover all their emotional needs in the language.

Much of our feeling, especially in English, is conveyed through intonation, and it is important for students to associate the intonation pattern with the feeling that gives rise to it. Moreover, what we say will be coloured not only by our feelings but by the mood and disposition of others. Drama techniques have the singular merit of directly engaging students' feelings and, as a result, often making them aware of the need to be able to express them appropriately.

Mood and feeling also influence the grammatical form of what we say. Take, for instance, a phrase such as 'It doesn't matter'. Depending on the sincerity of the speaker, this could emerge as 'never mind', 'don't bother', 'too bad', 'don't worry about it' (see 3.10 One-word dialogues and 3.11 Dialogue interpretation, for a development of this).

Shared knowledge

An important element in any 'real-life' situation is shared knowledge. Run your mind over the conversations you have in the course of a typical day. Nearly all of them involve unspoken assumptions, unconscious prejudices, or shared knowledge, which may never be referred to (see again 3.11). This is why the language of text-books often strikes us as being artificial. The early lessons in particular abound in expressions such as 'Mr Grey's house is big', 'His car is blue', 'The blue pencil is longer than the red one'. All the above remarks are possible, but only in a restricted context: they can be taken as examples of grammatical form, and learnt as such, but because they lack internal meaning, because they are immediately demonstrable and therefore self-evident, it is difficult for students to transfer what they have learnt from them to a situation in which they might conceivably be used. This brings us back to a point made earlier – that stating the obvious is not necessarily the best way of teaching 'simple' structures. Beginner's English should make as much sense as the language of advanced students. If, therefore, both you and I know that Mr Grey's house is big, there is little point in saying so. Our shared knowledge makes the remark superfluous.

All the above elements are present in a 'situation', though any one of them may predominate. A situation is a totality, and by extracting the verbal content to study it in isolation we risk losing or deforming the meaning. Drama can help us to restore this totality by reversing the learning process, that is, by beginning with meaning and moving to language from there.

About motivation

Much head-scratching goes on over the 'problem' of how to interest students in the language they are supposed to be learning. Many techniques have been tried – some crafty, some crude – to generate interest. Certain teachers believe that the only way is to let their students do what interests them most; often they come away disheartened: 'They aren't interested in anything', or 'They're never interested in the same thing'. Others try abandoning the text-book, but then 'The students feel they aren't learning anything'.

There can be no neat solution to motivation, but the 'problem' can be partly solved by asking, honestly, what those twenty or thirty people are trying to do *together* in the room. Surely, if communication is always on a one-to-thirty basis (i.e. from teacher to students), a great number of other possibilities are being wasted. A question from the teacher to one of the students is of direct interest to only two people in the class, though it may be of indirect interest to more. Drama helps us to keep all thirty people active all the time by making use of the dormant potential in the room. And, far from making the teacher's task harder, it actually relieves him or her of the burden of trying to do the impossible: keep thirty people active at the same intensity and at the same time. For, if the class is working in, say, five groups of six, the teacher's attention is split only in five ways and not thirty. The argument that the teacher can still not control what is happening in each group is surely spurious, for in facing the class he or she can control only one person at a time and cannot be aware of what is going on in the heads of the other twenty-nine except by constantly switching attention from one to another and keeping the students alert by cross-fire. Who then is doing *all* the work? The teacher. And what is he or she teaching?

Drama activities do not allow the teacher to gain a false sense of achievement by dispersing energy in all directions. They oblige him or her instead to stay on the edge of what is going on and not to crack the whip in the centre of the ring. They also help to get rid of the diffidence and boredom that come from being forced to stay passive most of the time. There is no place here for stereotyped responses, set-up discussions, pre-planned arguments or 'free conversations' in which everyone speaks and nobody listens, or else nobody speaks and the teacher is left to quench the fire started by his or her own burning questions. In a sense, motivation is not needed when working through drama, because the enjoyment comes from imaginative *personal* involvement, not from the sense of having successfully carried out someone else's instructions.

From the evidence to hand there is little doubt that these techniques are an extremely powerful motivational factor. Earl Stevick recently underlined the learner's need to feel a sense of 'belonging' (peer group acceptance) and security, and also to invest something of his own personality and so to enjoy a certain 'self esteem' (*Memory, meaning and method*, Newbury House 1976). The techniques fill precisely these needs.

If drama is motivating – and we believe it is – the reason may be that it draws on the entire human resources of the class and that each technique, in its own way, yields a different, unique, result every time it is practised. Nobody can predict what exactly will be thrown up in the way of ideas during these activities. This is what makes them enjoyable. We have, certainly, tried to predict some of the language that will be needed, but the language is only part of the activity. The other part is a compound of imagination, spontaneous creation and chance discovery, which depends on the students working together. An illustration of this is the apparently tightly-controlled exercise 3.18 The hotel receptionist, which offers little freedom of choice to the student 'performing' and yet regularly provides striking and entertaining new ideas, all based on the same stimulus – a single sentence on a slip of paper.

By working together, the students learn to feel their way to creating their own parts and adapting them as they come up against others. The problem of not wanting to speak or, more often, not knowing what to say is practically resolved because the activity makes it necessary to talk. One of the more obvious explanations for this is that the students are moving *physically*, as most of us are when we talk, which means that they can change partners and break away from exchanges that might begin to flag if they were kept up too long. Another reason is that they are learning to rely on one another for their ideas and therefore using a considerable amount of language for *discussion*, argument, agreement and disagreement, organization and execution.

It is interesting to listen to what is said at the beginning of most activities. Directive language will dominate for some time, 'You'd better...', 'I'll (lie on the ground) and you...', 'You begin, all right?' and so on. Once the skeleton of the activity has been built up, the *directive* language will be replaced by that of *discussion,* 'Wouldn't it be better if...?', 'I thought we were going to...', 'That won't work...'. This will be mixed in with whatever language may be involved in the sketch itself. In the final stage, we will have the language of *commentary* or *criticism*, as one of the groups tries to explain how it reacted to a sketch – 'Oh, we thought you were...', 'Weren't you...?', 'Why were you...?'.

This constant interchange is extremely difficult to achieve in a class where the focal point of the activity is often a text or a theme for discussion presented to a captive, seated audience. It is true that the language produced during many of the drama activities passes uncontrolled (by the teacher) and that most of what is said is heard by only two or three people, nevertheless, the whole class is actively engaged nearly all the time. Moreover, the words being 'wasted' on two or three pairs of ears are perhaps the most valuable, for every student needs periods in which to practise what he or she knows without restraint, without fear of being wrong. Students need the occasional chance to take risks in the language, to try out new ways of combining words, and of course, to find out where the gaps are in their knowledge. The drama activities give students an opportunity to strike a balance between fluency and accuracy.

Forbidden territory

Language teachers sometimes behave like the owners of large estates, putting up high walls round their territory and signs saying 'No Trespassing'. In secondary schools the foreign language becomes a subject on a timetable, and it is taught as a subject rather than as a language. As a result, the teacher of English shows little interest in what his or her colleagues might be doing in German or French; he or she may be on nodding terms with the teachers of Mathematics and History, and never have met the person in charge of Music or Science.

Drama is like the naughty child who climbs the high walls and ignores the 'No Trespassing' sign. It does not allow us to define our territory so exclusively: it forces us to take as our starting-point *life* not language. And life means all subjects, whether they are on the timetable or not. Drama may involve music, history, painting, mathematics, skiing, photography, cooking – anything. It does not respect subject barriers.

The language teacher will be wise to take advantage of this to enliven his or her work. Once students have discovered that there is another world, much closer and more real than that of Mr Brown, Herr Schmidt, and M. Dupont, with their waxwork wives and children, the problem of 'how to keep their interest' will gradually disappear. And, strangest of all, this other world does not need to be conjured up with expensive equipment – all that is needed is a roomful of human beings.

Some practical considerations

It would be difficult, and probably unwise, to try to base all your language work on activities such as those we describe here. It would be equally unwise, however, to base all your language work on a textbook. Any well-balanced course should be flexible enough to include various approaches to learning.

Most techniques for teaching any new item of language cover three major phases – presentation, practice, and reinforcement. In the first phase, one attempts to find a way of presenting the item so that it is clearly understood; in the second, one practises it under controlled conditions; and in the third, one tries to create conditions in which it can be used more or less freely by students. While dramatic activities can clearly play a part in the first two phases, it is really in the third phase that they come into their own. A judicious selection of such activities can certainly be used to reinforce particular items of vocabulary and structure, but their main advantage is in offering students the chance to move from controlled to free expression, and to say something they really want to say.

There is an alternative strategy in which the dramatic activity is done first and the communicative needs which are revealed are dealt with more systematically afterwards. Until you and your students are familiar with the techniques themselves, you may find it easier to adopt the first strategy.

As many of these activities may be unfamiliar at first, both to you and your students, it is best to introduce them as diversions. Try taking some of the early examples from Section 1 (*Introductory exercises*) and Section 2 (*Observation*) to begin with, since they make only modest demands on language and movement. For example, 2.3 Observation of the room, can at one level be used simply to reinforce certain items of vocabulary and structure (*door, window, wall, light, there's, there isn't, there are, there aren't*). Yet even at this relatively elementary level of language something more will be required if real interchange is to take place. This is why we have provided suggestions about the kind of language you may need to remind students of before they begin the exercises.

As your students gain confidence, and become used to the idea of being asked to *move round* in the room and make contact with the others in their group, you will be able to move on to some of the more demanding activities. Gradually you will be able to establish how much of your class time can be given over to an activity.

Language preparation

For activities like these, which are essentially student-based, some fairly general categories of language will be needed.

Transactional language, that is, the language needed for getting things done in a group situation, for example:

show me what you've got
it's my turn
give it to me
what did he say?
I'll be (the road-sign) you be (the motorist)
let's start again

Discussion language, which is used to come to agreement about something, to describe, comment on, or recall the activity in question:

he looks as if (he's holding something)
she might be (a magician)
I don't think so...
that's strange
I don't like that
Yes, of course
Oh no, perhaps not...
we thought it (might have been a tortoise)
we didn't understand (why you were sucking your thumb)

Performance language, which is the end product of some of these activities, but is in many senses the least important precisely because it involves the most preparation. Clearly, almost any language function can come into play here, depending on the nature of the activity.

We would suggest that transactional language, in particular, and to a lesser degree discussion language, should be made part of the more formal language learning activities from a very early stage. Without them it is not possible to operate at all. In other words, we suggest that it might be more profitable to teach items such as 'it's my turn', 'let's do it over here' right at the beginning of the course, rather than the more obvious but less immediately useful declarative statements such as 'this is a book'.

We have attempted to indicate *some* of the language which will be needed for each activity. Absolutely accurate prediction is impossible, but you will find that most activities do call heavily on one or two particular language functions. The presentation of this language can be done rapidly and informally. For instance, in an activity such as 2.17 Kim's game, which involves a good deal of *agreement* and *disagreement,* you might first set the students thinking by offering them several dogmatic statements about things familiar to them ('the post office is taller than the cathedral'; 'milk costs...'; 'our town is 84 km by road from the capital...'). They should react to these, agreeing or disagreeing, depending on how certain they are of the answers. At the end, you might write up six to ten common phrases expressing agreement and disagreement ('I don't think so'; 'No, it wasn't'; 'Quite right').

Certain activities may involve more careful preparation. If, for example, the students are likely to need to know *how to suggest an alternative course of action* (as in 3.22 Picture sets), they will need to know expressions such as:

wouldn't it be better if...?
I think we should...
let's try...
why don't we/doesn't he...?

In order to activate this language, you could first give them a few *communicative,* i.e. *meaningful,* drills. For instance, hand out a sheet with six simple line-drawings showing, for example, a man desperately trying to climb down a tree, with a ladder propped against the wall some distance away; a man using a hammer on the engine of his broken-down car. They are given the choice of two or three ways of commenting on these pictures to each other ('If I were him, I'd climb on to the wall'; 'Why doesn't he call for help?'; 'Wouldn't it be easier with a spanner?'). This then serves as a basis for the free use of these expressions in the drama activity.

Space

The traditional arrangement of chairs and tables or desks works against the successful use of dramatic activities. Ideally, the room should have no tables, and only a few chairs around the walls. If you cannot change the layout of your room, try to get another one; if this cannot be done, get the students to help you shift furniture out of the way. This may take time, but it is time well spent. Remember, too, that different activities require different arrangements. For some you need a completely open space, for others a semi-circle of chairs, and for others groups of chairs.

Why all this fuss about 'open space'? First, as will be immediately apparent, the activities require room because of the movement involved. Second, it is essential to be able to *see* who you are talking to, and to be able to move towards or away from him or her, to touch him or her or be touched. After all, when we talk we should be trying to communicate (not just 'answer questions'). How can you do this if all you can see is the backs of other people's heads?

The physical layout of the room reflects a psychological reality. For many people, rows of desks and chairs represent order and discipline; scattered groups of chairs or people squatting on the floor represent disorder and lack of control. This is one of the real reasons why many teachers oppose the idea of working in groups. They feel that the students have somehow escaped from their control and that this is, at least potentially, dangerous. This is not one of the objections which are publicly advanced; these are normally of the type, 'it takes too long to organize', 'they make too much noise', 'how can I correct them?', 'how can I give them the language they need?', 'how can I get them to talk English together?'. But such reasons for objecting are as often as not a reflection of the unease teachers feel at having the 'order' of the classroom upset.

The practical difficulties of working in this freer way can be greatly reduced by observing a few simple rules:

— before trying out a new activity ask the students to suspend judgement until it is over;
— give precise and unambiguous instructions for each activity; make sure students know who their partners are, which group they are working in, what they are expected to do;
— if materials (such as pictures, objects) are needed, make sure they are provided;
— keep close control over the time; avoid the temptation of letting an activity outgrow its own limitations: the saying that one should always leave the table feeling one could eat more is relevant here as well – it is better to stop too early than too late;
— decide what your own role is going to be; how much you are going to intervene (if at all).

The advantages of working in groups, pairs, or flexible groupings are enormous:

— the student-teacher relationship improves, because the teacher is no longer the 'fount of knowledge', he or she is the guide rather than the controller-in-chief;

- students talk more than before, and their exchanges are, as far as possible, 'natural';
- students participate in their own learning process;
- students gain from the sense of security offered by the group – individual talents are shared, everyone has a contribution to make, however small; weaker students often reveal unsuspected abilities, stronger students find themselves sharing what they know rather than trying to outdo their fellows.

The major difficulty which most teachers face, consciously or not, is how to transform the classroom from a space which is inherently inimical to learning into one where learning can take place. This problem is even greater for the language teacher: he or she needs to teach *communication* in a language, yet he is obliged to work in a classroom. The activities described in this book are one way of helping the teacher to overcome this problem.

When to stop

When an activity is going well it is tempting to let it run on unchecked. You will, however, find it best to cut it off somewhat prematurely. There will be cries of 'but we haven't finished yet!', but this should not worry you. The slight tension and frustration thus created often finds an outlet in talking *about* what was not done but might have been if they had been allowed to go on. So what you lose in 'performance' language is more than made up for by the language which emerges in these unplanned discussions.

With some of the more complex activities (for example in section 4 *Creation and invention*, and section 6 *Problem-solving*), you will need to allow enough time for free development to take place, but as a rule too much time spent on an activity leads to a slackening of pace and a loss of interest.

'Difficult customers'

There will always be one or two students who will not cooperate. Some will be genuinely shy, others will react to what they consider a waste of time, either by withdrawing or by over-participating, thus upsetting the work of the others.

There is no magic formula for dealing with difficult students of either type – the silent or the over-talkative. The best approach is, usually, to go on with your activity, paying no special attention to such students. Often the group itself will take care of the problem.

Shy students in particular gain confidence once they begin working in pairs or small groups, especially if they are given discreet encouragement or praise. Those who have decided to drop out often find themselves pressed to change their minds by others in their group.

Group pressures may also put down the student who wants to 'ham' or overdo everything. If this fails, you might try the reverse strategy: turn everyone's attention fully on him or her by saying, 'Oh, that was interesting, could you do it again for us all?' Obliged now to think about what he or she is doing, such a student often realizes that he or she cannot go on long in the same way.

Do not forget, however, that learning largely depends on the student's feeling of well-being and self-esteem. It is therefore better not to force students into roles in which they are acutely uncomfortable. Nearly always, if left to themselves, the members of a group will come up with or choose the roles which suit them best.

If there are times when you are worried by persistent non-cooperation by one or two students, remember that there will be non-participation with more traditional techniques as well – it is simply that such techniques make it easier to camouflage inactivity.

The use of the mother tongue

It is inevitable that students will at times revert to their own language. When we get excited, it is most natural for us to express this through our mother tongue.

When you begin trying to use the activities described in this book, do not stifle genuine reactions by insisting too heavily on the use of the foreign tongue. Let the activity develop. It often helps to keep students moving from group to group, as this prevents them from getting too deeply caught up in conversations in their own language. Even one student, sent round as a 'reporter' to each group, can have the effect of persuading them to use the foreign language.

With time, the students will come to associate the activities with the foreign tongue, and will have less difficulty in accepting its use. After all, they accept it in structural drills and comprehension exercises, so why not here? They know that they have come to learn the foreign language and it would be pointless not to use it. The decision by the students to use the foreign language instead of their own is a reflection of the confidence you have bred in them.

Student–teacher relationships

From all that has gone before, it must be clear that in order to use these techniques successfully there may have to be a radical change in the relationship between teacher and student. The activities cannot work unless there is a relaxed atmosphere. Rearranging the layout of the room will help, but you will also need to alter the students' idea, and possibly your own, of what the teacher is there for. You will no longer be the source of all knowledge nor the sole arbiter of what is 'right' and 'wrong', 'good' and 'bad'. Your main function now is to set things in motion; you are, to use the French word, the 'animateur'. You should ensure that the students understand what you want them to do, then step back as far as possible from what is happening, controlling but not directing.

It is tempting to want to intervene when you see something going 'wrong' or when a seemingly empty silence builds up. Resist the temptation. Periods of silence are necessary and natural; too hasty intervention deprives the student of the opportunity to reflect.

Remember, too, that in these activities there are no *wrong* ways of doing things, in the absolute sense. Grammatical mistakes there will be, but these can be dealt with in a more formal session. The students should be able to react and interact spontaneously, without feeling that they are to be penalized for being wrong. Unless they feel free to talk, they will not be able to give themselves fully to what they are doing. It is worth remembering that, even in your own language, you often need to say something two or three times in a group before the idea gets across, changing the way you express yourself each time. Your students will be doing the same. Encourage them to listen critically to each other's ideas; they will soon learn to pick up what is useful and discard what is irrelevant.

In brief, learn to withdraw, while making it clear that you are there when, and only when, you are needed.

We are aware that each activity will raise its own problems, in particular classroom organization, incorrect use of language, and being at a loss for words. This is why we have provided specific comments on each activity under the heading *Remarks*.

Level

An indication of the level of each activity is given in the *Remarks*. It is important to remember, however, that this is not a course-book and does not deal progressively with separate aspects of language. The activities presented here are designed for using rather than teaching the language. This means that the level of an activity is determined rather by the students' ability than by the exercise itself. To take an example, 3.18 The hotel receptionist can be performed effectively both by advanced students and by those with only a modest grasp of the language. If an exercise such as this is graded as elementary, it means that an elementary knowledge is *sufficient* to perform the activity. It does not mean that it is unsuitable for advanced students; far from it: advanced students will enjoy it at their own level.

The indication of level, therefore, is a guide to the minimum language requirements. It is not a definition of exclusive suitability.

The starring system used in the list of exercises below (pp. 32–7) is intended to complement the *Remarks* as a quick, easy reference guide to level. Here the system is outlined in a little more detail:

no star: suitable for all levels; little or no language required

* :   elementary – a modest vocabulary and the ability to use at least the present tenses

** :   intermediate – a working knowledge of the language; the ability to form simple sentences and to read short texts

*** : advanced – the ability to speak fluently and to read any text without undue difficulty

Note: These are, inevitably, broad categories. Certain of the activities can be performed at different levels, e.g. 4.14 Amazimbi or 2.14 If I remember rightly, by progressing from a simple to a more complex stage. Such exercises are marked with a star in brackets, e.g. (*)*, indicating that part of the activity will be suitable for more proficient learners. Explanations are given in the *Remarks* indicating how the levels can be adapted to the ability of the class.

Language needs

As we have seen, it is possible to predict at least some of the language a student will need to carry out a given activity. This is not, of course, to say that we can predict the precise sentences he or she may speak. But it is possible to say what he or she may need to *do* in the language: to describe or report facts, to ask for information, to make suggestions, to agree or disagree, and so on.

In working with these techniques we have identified eleven major categories of language acts which come up again and again. Not all of them will be necessary in every unit, and usually three or four will predominate. It may therefore be useful for you to have this list by you, so that you can check off possible language needs against it when you are preparing for a particular activity.

The questions you should ask yourself before beginning a new activity are:
- what will my students need to do in the language in order to carry out the activity successfully?
- which of the functions on the list will be called upon?
- what are some of the phrases they are likely to need to express these functions in this particular activity?

1 TALKING ABOUT FACTS

a) *Describing facts* (reporting, identifying) see 2.14 If I remember rightly...

There were two men in a hole.
The hole *was* in a dead-end street.
It was a sunny day.
One of them *had a* bowler hat on.
They were look*ing* around.

b) *Stating facts* (comparison, sequencing)

The explosion *came after* the shout.
The first one *was* louder.
There was a pause *before* the bottle was broken.

c) *Confirmation of facts* (emphasis)   see 2.17 Kim's game

You see, *it was* brown.
There aren't any marks on it.
It hasn't been open*ed*.
So, it did have a chain.

2 ELICITING INFORMATION

a) *General*   see 3.24 Tableaux

Were you on a bus?
What was that empty chair meant to be?
Why did she *keep* bend*ing* over you?
Was there someone hidden in the cupboard?

b) *Help or advice*   see 4.18 Act Three

What did he say?
I don't understand.
Can you help me with this chair?
Would it be better if I held it for you?
How can I lift it on my own?

c) *Comment*   see 3.17 What am I doing?

Where do you think I'm lying?
What am I hold*ing*?
Why aren't I mov*ing*?
Do you think my arm's broken?
Is (there) anyone with me?
How far away is he?
Could I move *if* I wanted to?

d) *Approval*   see 4.16 Making a machine

Is this *all right*?
Like this?
Would you like me *to* hold it?
Do you want me to do it again?

3 DIRECT QUESTIONING

a) *for Yes/No response*   see 2.16 Difficulty with large or small objects

> *You've got* glue on your hands.
> *Is that* glue you've got on your hands?
> *Have you* got glue on your hands?
> *Does it* feel sticky?
> *Are you* try*ing to* lift something?

b) *for identification*   see 3.4 What am I wearing?

> *Are you* an ice-hockey player?
> *Do you* work in a factory?
> *Can you* wear it at home?
> *Is this* something you wear at work?

c)   *for explanation*   see 3.29 Intruders

> *Why did you* drop your watch on the floor?
> *What was* the thing floating in the swimming pool?
> *Where were* you supposed to be?

d)   *for clarification*   see 3.18 The hotel receptionist

> *So, you haven't* got a headache?
> *But you want* an aspirin for someone who has?
> *The* person *is* in your room, *isn't* he?
> *He's* feel*ing* sick?
> *Because* he had too much to drink?
> *Then you want* me to give you an aspirin for your husband who got a hangover?
> *It's* your husband, *isn't it*?

4 SEEKING CONFIRMATION   see 3.21 Bringing a picture to life

a) *as an interpretation of a fact or action*

> *You've been* wallpapering, *haven't you*?
> *Sombody's* phon*ed*?
> *I think* you were having breakfast and...
> *You must have* left the razor-blade there by mistake...
> *It's a* sack of potatoes, *surely*?
> *Couldn't you be* queu*ing* for the hovercraft?

b) *in response to a)*

> *That's right, yes...*
> *Quite right.*
> *Absolutely.*
> *That's it.*
> *Right.*
> *Certainly.*   Yes/No response
> *No, definitely not.*
> *Not at all.*
> *Oh, no!*
> *Wrong.*
> *I'm afraid not.*
>
> *Well, perhaps...*
> *In a way...*
> *Not really...*
> *Could be...*   Indefinite or vague
> *It depends...*
> *It might (be) I suppose...*
> *Sort of.*
>
> *Almost...*
> *Not quite...but...*
> *In a way / sense...*
> *Yes...Yes*   Encouraging
> *But what else?*
> *Not bad. You're nearly there.*
> *You're on the right track.*

5 STATEMENT OF OPINION (+ JUSTIFICATION) see 3.22
Picture sets

> *It looks to me as if* they're expecting an explosion.
> *I think they're* bird watchers.
> *I have the impression* it's a trick photograph.
> *What I think has happened is that* they've lost the key.
> *I feel* they must have a reason for being there.

see 2.10 Listening with eyes closed

> *It couldn't have been* a cow-bell *because* there are no cows here.
> *I don't think it was* an electric saw – *it wasn't* even *enough.*
> *I don't think it was* a window breaking, *otherwise* somebody
> would have shouted.

6 EXPRESSION OF CERTAINTY OR UNCERTAINTY see 2.5
Spot the change and 2.17 Kim's game

It was blue. I'm sure of that.
It definitely wasn't green.
I'm sure it was red.
I'm certain it wasn't pink.
It can't have been made of silver.
It must have been gold.
I don't think it was a bus-ticket.
I seem to remember a hole in it.

7 SUGGESTING See 4.10 Rules of the game

a) *Making suggestions or proposals*

Let's form a circle.
Why don't we stand in a row?
We could try using a net.
How / what about moving like this?
Couldn't we do it faster?
Wouldn't it be a good idea to start again?
I think we should change places.
I suggest / propose doing the turning bit before the bending
bit.

b) *Rejecting suggestions and raising objections*

No.
That's no good.
We can't do that.
I'm not so sure about that.
I don't think that's a very good idea.
I don't agree.
How can we possibly do that?
Are you serious?
You must be joking.

c) *Accepting suggestions or proposals*

Good idea!
Why not?
All right then.
Fine.
O.K. I don't mind trying.

8 COMMENTING (ON OTHER PEOPLE'S ACTIONS) see 3.24
Tableaux and 3.27 Conflict

a) *Neutral*

> *It wasn't bad* (I suppose)
> *Not bad*
> It was / *all right*
>   / *O.K.*
>   / *interesting*

b) *Favourable*

> *Great*!
> *Marvellous*!
> *Well done*!
> That was / *fine*
>   / *very good*
>   / *very well acted*
> *I liked*   / the end
>   / the way you fell down
> *What I liked best was* the way she looked so bored.

c) *Unfavourable*

> That was / *awful*
>   / *rotten*
>   / *no good at all*
> *That wasn't very* interesting, I'm afraid.
> *I didn't enjoy* it at all.
> *I didn't like* the way you pushed him.
> *Why didn't you* put more life into it?
> *Couldn't you have* looked older?
> *I can't understand why* she didn't play the mother.

9 SELF-CORRECTION AND REFORMULATION see 3.28
Tension

a) *Expressing self-correction*

> *You're* in a bus, *no not* a bus, *a* taxi?
> Perhaps you're sitting in a theatre. Or *wait a minute perhaps*
>   *it's a* cinema. *Maybe I'm wrong.* Maybe it's a train.
> *No, just a minute. It can't be* a radio, *it must be* a bomb.
> *No, I didn't mean* a typist, *I meant* a secretary.
> No. *What I wanted to say* was a nuisance.

b) *Encouraging reformulation*

Are you sure?
A radio?
You're sure he's a gambler *are you?*
Not angry *exactly.*
But what else?

c) *Responding to a) and b)*

Well, sort of.
In a way, yes.
Well a kind of an expert.

10 GIVING DIRECTIVES   see 4.18 Act Three

(Now) you be the waiter. *(O.K.?)*
Don't stand there, sit down.
I want you to pretend you haven't noticed.
Here's what I want you to do.
What I'd like you to do is to look away from her.
Let's try it once again.
Why doesn't he play the waiter?

11 EXPRESSING AGREEMENT AND DISAGREEMENT   see 4.13
Starting from scratch

a) *Enthusiastic agreement*

Good idea!
Fine.
I quite agree.
O.K. then.
Great!

b) *Reluctant agreement*

I don't mind.
All right then.
If you like.
I suppose so.

c) *Disagreement*

No.
Impossible.
I disagree.

We can't do that.
Definitely *not*.
I'm not / too sure / happy / *about that*.
Do you really think so?
I don't know about that.
That's not a very good idea.
Can't you think of anything better?

d) *Seeking agreement*

Does everyone agree?
All right then?
O.K.?
Is that all right *then?*
Well shall we choose a spade *then?*
How many of you agree?
Is everyone happy about the idea of a waiter?

List of exercises indicating language requirements

(Stars indicate minimal language requirements: no star – little or no language required, * elementary, ** intermediate, *** advanced. Bracketed stars indicate that part of the activity can be performed at a different level. For a further description of level, see pp. 22–3 above.)

1 Introductory exercises

Warming-up exercises

Non-verbal cooling-down exercises

2 Observation

3 Interpretation

4 Creation and invention

5 Word-play

6 Problem-solving

7 The use of literary texts, poems and songs

8 A day's work

Outline of a typical day's concentrated work, with comments on the choice, function and order of individual exercises.   225

1 Introductory exercises

Many of the exercises which follow are non-verbal, and a word of explanation is perhaps necessary in a book which is, after all, about language.

Why bother with exercises which take up time and lead to little, if any, use of the foreign language? The reasons given here are not exhaustive, but they are the principal ones:

1 These exercises help to mark off clearly what has gone before from what is to come, or they serve as a smooth liaison between activities. It is unrealistic (though unhappily it only too often occurs) to expect students to come from a lesson in another subject, such as maths, or from another activity, such as a day at the office, and start immediately on 'learning' the foreign language. Nor is it realistic to switch abruptly from one activity to another within a lesson or session. These exercises help to wipe out such immediate worries and concerns.

2 They are also intended to put the students in a relaxed, uninhibited state in which they are much more receptive than they would otherwise be. This lowering of the threshold of unconscious resistance to learning the foreign language makes for more open, creative working in subsequent exercises.

3 Many, though not all, lead to an increase in awareness of others, and of oneself in relationships with others. The confidence engendered in this way makes possible the cooperative learning which many of the other exercises demand.

The exercises described here are by no means all that could be done. Indeed, we hope they will give you ideas for developing further exercises of a similar kind which suit your students and your style of teaching.

For the sake of convenience only, the exercises have been divided into four kinds: non-verbal warming-up exercises, non-verbal relaxation/cooling-down exercises, verbal exercises, and group-formation exercises.

Clearly, exercises like these cannot be graded in any strict sense. We have, however, presented them in groupings where there are common elements between exercises.

Exactly how you choose to use them will depend very much on

the 'feel' of the class at any given moment. Do they need warming up, or cooling down? Will one exercise be enough, or do they need two or three (Monday mornings! Friday afternoons!)? Necessarily, you will only find the ideal mix by your experience of using them. You will also come to have a feel for the ones which serve as good introductory exercises to some of the longer, more sustained activities suggested later in this book.

You may like to look at section 8 to see how a day's work (or a series of sessions) might be organized.

NON-VERBAL WARMING-UP EXERCISES

1.1   Handshakes (1)

What to do

Everyone walks freely about the room. The object is to shake hands with everyone in the room, without speaking, but with an appropriate facial expression. (Instructions may be given which involve a change in expression, e.g. 'Each person you shake hands with is a very good friend', or 'You are at a very formal reception, you do not know any of the people you meet', etc.)

Remarks

Suitable for all levels.

   This extremely simple activity has the virtue of getting the students on the move and making some sort of contact with *everyone* else in the room. The physical contact of the handshake is clearly of symbolic importance as a gesture of mutual goodwill. The eye-contact established each time is no less important. This is a good starting exercise with groups who are meeting for the first time.

See also 1.35 Handshakes (2).

1.2   Hand catching

What to do

In pairs, students stand facing each other. One person holds out both hands, about 25 cm apart. The other person tries to pass a hand vertically between his or her partner's hands without getting caught in the trap, which can of course close at any time. When a hand is caught, the partners reverse roles.

Remarks

Suitable for all levels.

This exercise gets rid of a lot of nervous energy which could otherwise get in the way of the more sustained exercises. People of all ages play the game with great gusto and tend to forget themselves in it. It also rapidly establishes a relationship, partly physical, with another person.

One useful ploy is to ask students to change partners two or three times in a five-minute period.

See also 1.41 Gift of the gab.

1.3 Mirror hands

What to do

Students stand facing each other in pairs with their hands raised to shoulder height, palms facing outward, and as close as possible to their partners' *without* actually touching.

One student is the 'leader', and begins to move both hands in a plane, i.e. always keeping the palms facing outward no matter in which direction the hands are moved. His or her partner has to follow as accurately as possible, as if in a mirror. Both students in each pair should have a turn at being 'leader'.

Remarks

Suitable for all levels.

This exercise demands a very high degree of concentration. The need to anticipate someone else's body movement is analogous to the sort of anticipation demanded in verbal exchanges. The activity usually develops a high degree of eye-contact between partners.

In some cases it may be necessary to stress that this is a cooperative not a competitive activity.

See also 1.4 Hand touching.

1.4 Hand touching

What to do

Students stand facing each other in pairs with their hands raised to shoulder height and palms touching.

They are told to move their hands slowly in as many different ways as possible without losing palm contact.

After a few minutes, the pairs become threes and continue the exercise. After a few more minutes, the threes should become fours, still continuing the same exercise.

Remarks

Suitable for all levels.

Here, too, a great deal of concentration is called for, as well as physical effort in cases where students try out difficult and complex movements. The fact of being literally 'in touch' with another person, or with other persons, in the carrying out of a cooperative movement is important in developing the sense of reciprocal confidence needed for the more demanding linguistic exercises.

A useful verbal follow-up is to ask students the differences they feel between doing the exercise in twos, in threes, in fours. Which was easiest? Most comfortable? Which gave the most interesting visual results?

1.5 Numbers in your head

What to do

Each person finds a space to stand in. With eyes closed, everyone traces the shape of the numbers from 0–9 by moving their heads only (i.e. no movement of the trunk).

Then one person is appointed to call out numbers, which everyone makes the same way, still with eyes closed (e.g. 29, 57, 233, etc.).

Finally, in pairs facing each other, one person makes a number, and the other tries to guess what it is – eyes open this time! (This last stage involves a little language.)

Remarks

Some minimal language required.

Apart from being an excellent exercise for the neck and throat muscles, this involves a high degree of concentration. It also helps students to 'feel' the physical shape of the numbers in the foreign language. It is arguable whether this physical representation of the numbers helps in fully internalizing them in the foreign language – a difficult task, even for advanced students. (It is, moreover, well known that the ability to count and reckon with ease in the foreign language is rare, even among fluent speakers.)

In the last part of the exercise, purposeful cooperative interaction is beginning.

See also 1.6 Body numbers.

1.6 Body numbers

What to do

Students need enough space to be able to extend their arms freely without touching anyone else. One person is appointed to call out numbers between 0 and 9. As a number is called, students try to form the shape of it using their whole bodies. The shape should be held until another number is called.

In pairs, students form two-digit numbers (e.g. 22, 75, 83, etc.) for other pairs to interpret.

Remarks

Some minimal language required.

This is clearly an excellent physical exercise involving many un-pedagogical muscles! The concentration it requires usually makes people forget the possibly 'ridiculous' shapes they are forming. Everyone is so intent on the task that there is no time to look at others (except in the pair work, where the looking has a real object).

The pair work is again a good way in to more complex activities.

1.7 Sounds with the right shape

What to do

A recording of sounds (e.g. squeal of brakes, screeching of gulls, washing of waves, etc.) or of brief musical extracts (e.g. African drums, a gong, flute solo, etc.) is needed. As the sound or extract is played, students make themselves into a shape which seems to them appropriate. With more advanced students, it is worthwhile discussing why a certain shape was adopted.

The exercise can also be done in a group. For this to work properly, the recording must be played first, then time left for the groups to discuss the figure they will form. The recording is played again when they actually make the figure.

Remarks

Some minimal language required.

Like exercise 1.6, this is an excellent physical loosening-up exercise, involving the gradual loss of self-consciousness in the absorption of the task.

See also 1.28 Slow motion, 2.2 Freeze!

1.8   Remaking the web

What to do

Everyone finds a space to be in, either lying, sitting or standing, according to choice. Whatever their posture, everyone should be touching two other people, either with hands, feet, or head, so that the pattern seen from above looks like a web or network. Students observe carefully where they are in relation to their neighbours, and the exact position they are in. Everyone then stands up and changes position, mixing up with the others. When the word is given, the web has to be remade as exactly as possible.

Remarks

Suitable for all levels.

Again, the advantage is physical contact between students performing a cooperative task.

See also 2.2 Freeze!, 4.9 Statues.

1.9   Falling

What to do

Each person finds a space big enough to turn round in with arms extended and without touching anyone else. With eyes closed, students are asked to let themselves fall to the floor and to remain in the position in which they fall, with eyes still closed.

They are then asked to think about the various parts of the body – arms, hands, legs, feet, head, etc. – and how they feel. Are they in a normal or an unusual position, tense/relaxed, etc.? Discussion can follow with eyes open.

Remarks

Suitable for all levels.

Obviously not an exercise to be done on marble or cement floors! Falling is a supremely self-confident thing to do, especially 'blind'. You may find that some people fall very gingerly to begin with, barely sagging to their knees and rolling daintily sideways. Remember you cannot force someone to fall without fear. It may help to ask students to imagine they have been shot in a gangster film; this gives them a mental image to which they can approximate.

The second part of the exercise – making oneself conscious of how different parts of the body feel – is equally important, and the discussion can be both fascinating and useful purely as language learning. (What do you call '*un ginocchio*'? etc.)

See also the following three exercises.

1.10 Swings

What to do

Groups of eight are needed. Seven people form the swing and the eighth lies in it, supported at the neck, the armpits, the waist and the knees.

The group then gently swings the reclining member backwards and forwards. Everyone has a turn in the swing.

With students already trained in mutual confidence, the same exercise can be done with the eighth student falling backwards into the waiting cradle.

Remarks

Suitable for all levels.

The exercise is valuable in developing confidence between and among group members. It also involves cooperation in caring for a group member. Besides these advantages, the exercise is extremely relaxing and enjoyable for the person in the swing!

With more boisterous groups, it may be necessary to emphasize the need for *gentle* handling and for slow regular movement.

See also 1.11 See-saw, 1.12 Roundabouts.

1.11 See-saw

What to do

Students form pairs. One partner stands behind the other. The one in front then falls backwards, preferably with eyes closed, and is caught by his or her partner and returned to the upright position. After several falls, partners change places.

The same exercise should then be done with partners facing each other.

A further variation is done in threes, with the middle person being rocked *gently* between the other two. All three should have a turn in the middle.

Remarks

Suitable for all levels.

It is important that the person falling should remain straight, like a tree-trunk, when falling. At the beginning, those doing the catching should stand fairly near the one falling. With increased confidence in their ability to catch, they can move progressively farther away. It is important to stress to those falling that they *will* be caught, and have nothing to worry about.

The exercise clearly promotes both self-confidence and mutual confidence, both of them qualities useful for the creative activities suggested later in this book.

1.12   Roundabouts

What to do

Groups of about eight people stand in a circle, with one of them in the middle. He or she should stand with arms folded and eyes closed. The circle closes in to about 30 cm away from this person, and everyone in it raises their hands to shoulder height with palms facing outwards.

The person in the middle then falls in any direction. He or she must not be allowed to fall, but should instead be pushed gently around the circle (it is important that the person falling should remain straight and fall like a tree-trunk, not simply rock from the hips). Everybody should have a turn in the middle.

Remarks

Suitable for all levels.

Like the previous two exercises, this develops a strong sense of mutual confidence and cooperation. This physical trust is, in our view, an important prerequisite for the psychological trust involved in free, creative interactions.

The students will again need to be reassured that no harm will come to anyone. It is usually necessary to circulate among groups to check that those in the middle are really 'letting go' and that *gentleness* prevails.

See also 1.23 Blind, 1.52 Leading the blind, 2.18 Lost memory.

1.13 Jumping Janus

What to do

In pairs, standing back-to-back, students lock elbows. In turn, they lift each other slowly off the ground and back again.

Remarks

Suitable for all levels.

Good for getting rid of surplus energy and as an exercise in cooperation. It is useful to change partners several times in the course of the activity.

See also 4.9 Statues.

1.14   Eels in the grotto

What to do

Students should form groups of eight to ten people. One person is chosen as an 'eel'. The rest of the group form themselves into a 'grotto' (i.e. a shape with lots of holes in it – see diagram).

The 'eel' then has to wriggle through all the holes in the 'grotto'. Every member of the group has a turn as 'eel'.

Remarks

Suitable for all levels.

Apart from being quite a demanding physical exercise, we know of no better way of having everyone touching everyone else. But the emphasis is not on the touching: it is on getting through all those holes. The taboo on touching is not invoked, since attention is focussed elsewhere.

This is not, however, an exercise to be done early on in the history of a class. It is better to wait until students are thoroughly used to working together.

See also 4.9 Statues.

1.15 Underneath the arches

What to do

The whole class forms a circle holding hands. One person breaks the circle and starts to weave in and out between the people, followed by those behind. A fabulous knot of writhing humanity usually results.

Remarks

Suitable for all levels.
    A simpler form of 1.14 Eels in the grotto which does not require the preparation of a 'grotto', but is correspondingly less demanding. It can be done relatively early in a programme.

1.16 Catch!

What to do

In pairs, students throw an imaginary ball to and fro between them. Details about the kind of ball can be given to make the mime more concrete, e.g. 'You are throwing a tennis ball/football/ medicine ball (i.e. a very heavy ball tossed and caught for exercise), a balloon, etc.'
    A possible variation is to have the partners playing imaginary table tennis.

Remarks

Suitable for all levels.
    Emphasis should be placed on the need to really feel and see the imagined ball – its size, weight, etc. Both partners should be able to follow it with their eyes as it is thrown. It is important that the exercise should not be seen as trivial and made banal. To be done well, it needs total commitment to the action, so that an outsider too can 'see' what is not there.

See also 3.17 What am I doing?, 4.10 Rules of the game.

1.17 Tug-o'-war

What to do

An equal number of teams of about six people is needed. Each team appoints a leader who faces the leader of another team. The teams line up behind their leader.

An imaginary rope is held between both teams. At the word 'go', each team tries to pull the opposing team over a line.

Remarks

Suitable for all levels.

To succeed, this needs a good deal of reciprocal anticipation by the members of both teams. The rope has really to be perceived and felt, and the ebb and flow of strength from one side to the other needs real concentration. It is made pointless if both teams simply walk backwards away from each other!

See also 3.17 What am I doing?, 4.10 Rules of the game.

1.18 Maestro

What to do

Material needed: a recording of orchestral music, preferably something with a strongly marked tempo (e.g. Saint-Saens, 'Carnival of the animals', Carl Orff, 'Carmina Burana', Stravinsky, 'The Rite of Spring', Purcell, 'Funeral music for Queen Mary'). Each student imagines himself or herself as the conductor of the orchestra, and 'conducts' the extract. (It often helps if this is done with eyes closed.)

A variation is for students to choose one of the instruments involved in the extract and to mime playing it. In some groups, this will lead on to the formation of an 'orchestra' which will be conducted by one (or more) of the students.

Remarks

Suitable for all levels.

This works equally well for warming up and cooling down, depending very much on the piece of music chosen.

See also 1.38 Becoming a musical instrument, 1.19 Beat out that rhythm, 1.28 Slow motion.

1.19 Beat out that rhythm

What to do

Students sit on the floor in a big circle. One person starts to beat out a regular rhythm on the floor (or by clapping hands, clicking fingers, etc.) The next person adds in a variation on the rhythm, then the next person, and so on until a composite beat results.

Variations are to build up to a climax and fade away to a scarcely audible beat.

Remarks

Suitable for all levels.

This requires considerable self-control (in keeping the overall noise level down so that later variations can be perceived as they are added) and concentration (in holding on to one's own beat in spite of all the others going on nearby).

It is better done with groups of up to twelve. If a class of thirty is involved, it is better to subdivide into three groups of ten, each of which performs separately.

See also 4.14 Amazimbi, 7.6 What's in a name?

1.20   **What we feel like**

What to do

Students form pairs. Several minutes are given so that each person can discover what his or her partner feels like: the texture of his or her clothes, hair, and skin; the shape of his or her hands, height, girth, etc. Students then close their eyes, or are blindfolded, and mixed up around the room. The object is for partners to find each other again by touch only. (No speaking is allowed.)

Remarks

Suitable for all levels.

Obviously, care has to be taken not to allow this to turn into a 'group-grope', and there may be groups where national or religious injunctions make it difficult or impracticable. However, in our experience, provided the organizer presents it tactfully, with emphasis on the finding, not on the feeling, there is no fear of it going sour. Clearly, it is not for the first session in a new group, and should only be done after some of the milder warming-up exercises are already familiar.

See also 1.23 Blind, 4.5 Cork, stone and wood.

1.21   **You touch my back, I'll touch yours!**

What to do

Students stand facing each other in pairs. They put their left hands behind their backs, palm facing outwards. The object is for each person to try to touch his or her partner's left hand with his or her own right hand – and of course to avoid being touched by the other person!

Remarks

Suitable for all levels.

This tends to be a rather hectic activity and is best done for a short time only. Like 1.2 Hand catching, it releases nervous energy through physical movement and contact.

As with many of the pair-work activities, it is often useful to ask students to change partners once or twice in the course of the exercise.

1.22   Touch it

What to do

Students are grouped in the middle of the room. They are then asked to touch a variety of objects, surfaces, colours, textures, etc. (e.g. 'Touch something yellow...something rough...something round, etc.')

Remarks

Suitable for all levels.

A good mixer. Helpful, too, in getting students to observe their environment carefully.

See also 4.5 Cork, stone and wood, 2.3 Observation of the room.

1.23   Blind

What to do

The room is scattered with obstacles, e.g. chairs. Students form pairs. One is blindfolded (or has eyes closed); the other guides the 'blind' partner silently and carefully about the room by holding his or her arm. No speaking is allowed. Partners then change roles, and repeat the exercise. If there is time, change partners and repeat the exercise.

Remarks

Suitable for all levels.

A very good exercise for developing confidence between members of a group.

See also 1.52 Leading the blind.

NON-VERBAL COOLING-DOWN EXERCISES

1.24 Breathing

What to do

a) The students stand in their own space, close their eyes and breathe in deeply. Then release breath slowly. Each time, the period during which the breath is held should be lengthened. (It helps if, after taking in a lungful of air, a little bit is released before holding the breath.)

b) The same exercise, this time as they exhale the students sing a given note for as long as they can.

c) The same as in b), but this time the note starts strong and gradually fades away. Alternatively, it can start weak and rise to a crescendo (though this is more difficult).

d) The same, but with two groups. One starts strongly and gradually fades away, the other starts weakly and builds up to a climax. All on the same note.

Remarks

Suitable for all levels.

Apart from being good exercises in controlling the breathing, they also develop concentration and produce a feeling of pleasant relaxation.

Keeping eyes closed may seem fanciful, but it does help to restore inward calm.

1.25 Feeling my space

What to do

Ideally, this should be done in a room where students can lie comfortably on the floor, with eyes closed. They should be told to feel the space they occupy, then gradually to expand into it as far as their limbs and bodies will extend. Then gradually to contract back into the space, occupying as little of it as possible.

Remarks

Suitable for all levels.

Instructions should be given in a calm yet firm voice.

The effect of the exercise is often equivalent to a good sleep.

If physical conditions do not allow for using the floor to lie on, the exercise can still be done – though less satisfactorily – by simply sitting on chairs.

See also 1.26 Feeling your muscles, 1.27 From seed to plant, 7.9 Amnesty.

1.26 Feeling your muscles

What to do

a) Ideally, this is done with students lying comfortably on the floor in their own space, with eyes closed. When the word is given, they tense *all* their muscles and hold them tense until told to relax again. This is done several times. The students are then left to lie quietly for a few moments before getting up.

b) A variant is to ask everyone to go completely floppy. (The organizer can check this by picking up the odd hand or leg to see if there is any muscular tension.) Then the organizer tells everyone to start slowly to tense their muscles, beginning from the toes and working gradually upwards until the whole body is tensed. The muscles should be relaxed progressively from head to toe. Again, the students should be left a little time to lie quietly before they get up.

Remarks

Suitable for all levels.

This exercise has the effect of concentrating attention on little-used or forgotten muscles. Besides being a pleasant, relaxing activity, it also serves to 'tune up' the body for exercises in which physical movement leads to language. As, for instance, in the various mime exercises, particularly 3.2. Things aren't what they seem to be, 3.17 What am I doing?, 3.18 The hotel receptionist, 4.13 Starting from scratch.

See also 1.25 Feeling my space, exercises 1.27–1.30, section 8 A day's work.

1.27 From seed to plant

What to do

The students stand in their own space. They are asked to curl up, making themselves as small as they possibly can. When the word is given, they are to uncoil *very slowly* into a plant stretching up towards the sun.

Remarks

Suitable for all levels.

Again, concentration, awareness of the body, and muscular control are involved. Like the previous exercise, this activity is directly linked to the mime exercises, particularly those in which transformations (of space or of objects) are suggested by the body, e.g. 2.16 Difficulty with large or small objects and 7.9 Amnesty, and in all exercises where the language produced depends on the *interpretation* of movement.

Any piece of music which begins slowly and softly and builds up to a climax can be used to accompany the exercise. The symphonies of Mahler, Sibelius and Brahms are particularly suitable, but jazz or electronic music might also be used.

See also exercises 1.25–1.30.

1.28 Slow motion

What to do

The students form pairs. The room needs to be cleared. A recording of some suitably slow music should be played (see below for suggestions). The students move to the music together, but in slow motion (not just slowly, but really in slow motion, as in the slowed-down shots of athletes).

Remarks

Suitable for all levels.

Excellent for developing muscular control and awareness of shared space. Ideal as a preliminary exercise for activities in which the language depends on close observation of gesture and movement, e.g. 3.18 The hotel receptionist, 3.20 Becoming a picture, 3.24 Tableaux.

The class may need to be reminded at first that the purpose is to move *as slowly as possible*. It is also worth remembering that, because the exercise is done in silence, it might be followed by any of the word-play activities in section 5.

See also 1.7 Sounds with the right shape, 4.16 Making a machine, section 8 A day's work.

SUGGESTIONS FOR MUSIC

Richard Strauss, 'Vier letzte Lieder'; Mahler, 'Fifth symphony', 'Kindertotenlieder'; Dvorak, 'Violin concerto' (adagio); Beethoven, 'Piano concerto no. 3' (largo); 'Piano concerto no. 5' (adagio), and certain of the piano sonatas; Wagner, main theme from 'Tristan and Isolde'; Purcell, 'Funeral music for Queen Mary'; Ravel, 'Pavane pour une enfante défunte', 'Piano concerto for the left hand', second movement; Handel, 'Largo'; Schubert, 'String quintet in C' / D. 956/, second movement; Brahms, 'Piano concerto no. 2', second movement; much modern electronic music would also be suitable.

1.29 Relax!

What to do

These exercises can be done either sitting or lying down; they must, however, be done with the eyes closed. Any of the following instructions can then be given (or any others which work!).

a) Imagine you are under a luxurious warm shower after a long, tiring day. Feel the water running all over you, washing away all the fatigue.
b) Sit comfortably. Now begin to rock from side to side very slowly. Hum a tune.
c) Sit comfortably. Use your right hand to stroke your left hand, very slowly. Now stroke your arms, also very slowly.
d) Imagine that you can see in front of you an endless piece of black velvet. Concentrate on it.
e) Look at this diagram. Then close your eyes and try to see it in your mind's eye. Concentrate on it.

   or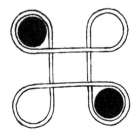

Remarks

Level: elementary upwards.

The reason for insisting on eyes closed is to cut off external distraction and to drive each student inward to concentrate on his or her own state of consciousness. If a great deal of resistance to these ideas is encountered, it is best not to insist; one of the other exercises should be done instead, and these ideas can be tried again some other time.

1.30 Directed relaxation

What to do

Ideally, students should be lying comfortably on the floor in their own space, with eyes closed. The exercise can, however, be done from a seated position.

The organizer should speak in a soft, calm, unhurried but firm voice. 'You are full of energy. It is like a fluid in your body. Try to feel it in your toes. Feel it moving very slowly, flowing into your feet, your ankles. Now it is flowing, spreading, very slowly up your legs...' and so on, until the head. 'Now you have a small hole at the back of your head. Feel all the energy draining away through the hole. Slowly, slowly. Now rest.' When the exercise is over, students should sit up slowly, in their own time.

Remarks

Level: elementary upwards.

The voice quality is most important. It is also essential not to hurry, leaving plenty of time for students to feel each part of themselves.

1.31 Listening

What to do

The students all sit or lie with eyes closed. The organizer reads (or plays a recording of) a story or better still a poem. Preferably something with a slow, soothing, rhythmic beat. (For instance, D.H. Lawrence, 'Kangaroo'; Robert Frost, 'Stopping by woods on a snowy evening'; Oscar Wilde, 'Requiescat' – 'Tread lightly, she is near, under the snow...'; Gerard Manley Hopkins, 'Spring and Fall: to a young child'; Browning, 'My Last Duchess'; Keats, 'La Belle Dame sans Merci', 'Ode to Autumn'; Coleridge, 'The Rime of the Ancient Mariner'; Fitzgerald, 'The Rubaiyat of Omar Khayyam' etc.)

Remarks

Level: intermediate upwards.

Again, voice quality is the key to success.

It is *not* important that students understand all they hear, since it is the rhythm and voice quality to which they are listening.

One possible variation is to prepare a recording of one or more sentences which are repeated over and over again. Some ideas are given below.

See also 7.6 What's in a name?

IDEAS FOR REPEATED SENTENCES

1 We have time.
  Time is something we have.
  Plenty of time.
  All the time in the world.
  Time unending.
  Time is on our side.
  Time is standing still.
  We have time.
  All the time in the world.
  Plenty of time.
  Time unending.
  Time is standing still. etc.

2 Other possibilities, on the theme of 'calm', 'quiet':

  It is quiet.
  So quiet.
  No noise.
  Not a sound etc.

  All is still.
  Very still.
  The stillness is everywhere.
  All over. etc.

1.32 Rediscovering the circle

What to do

If there is room, the whole class forms one big circle. If not, smaller circles are formed. Everyone stands with eyes closed, and holding hands. When the word is given, everyone starts to walk, *very slowly*, towards the centre of the circle, until the whole group is concentrated there. This must be done very gently and with no pushing or shoving. Then, equally slowly, everyone walks backwards (still with eyes closed) to re-form the original circle.

Remarks

Suitable for all levels.

If done properly, this gives a sense of group solidarity and consideration. It involves people in physical contact, but not for the sake of it.

A good cooling-down exercise after a more hectic activity.

See also 2.18 Lost memory, 1.52 Leading the blind.

1.33 Don't break it!

What to do

The students stand in circles of about ten. They are asked to imagine that a very large, fragile plate is in the centre of their circle. They have to pick it up and carry it carefully to another part of the room.

Remarks

Suitable for all levels.

This involves a high degree of group concentration and coordination if done well. It also involves awareness of shared space, since several groups will want to move at the same time.

See also section 8 A day's work.

1.34   Find a seat

What to do

Chairs are placed around the edges of the room. Everyone is seated. When the word is given they move to the centre of the room, turn to face their chairs, close eyes, and walk carefully back to their chairs and sit down again (without touching the chair before sitting). This should be done several times.

Remarks

Suitable for all levels.

A good exercise for developing concentration and awareness of space and distance. It instantly creates an atmosphere of quiet concentration.

If there are too many in the class, it may help to have students working in pairs, one standing behind the chair to help his or her partner if necessary.

VERBAL EXERCISES

The language associated with these activities is of two kinds: language inherent in the activity (e.g. the sentences written on people's backs in 1.43 Backs), and that used for comment and discussion. In most of these activities, both kinds of language can be varied to suit the language level of the group. As students advance in proficiency, one would expect the comment and discussion to become more important.

1.35   Handshakes (2)

What to do

The students move freely about the room shaking hands with *everyone* else. As they do so, they say their own first names. They then do the same exercise again, only this time they have to greet the other person by name. If they cannot remember, the other person should help them.

A variation is to set the occasion for the meeting/greeting (e.g. this is a reunion party of old friends who have not seen each other for ten years, or this is at the funeral of a very good friend, etc.). As they shake hands, the students should make appropriate remarks.

Remarks

Suitable for all levels.

A good exercise for getting the class mixed up and in some kind of brief physical contact. It is one of the exercises which helps everyone to learn everyone else's name – an important factor in loosening up formal relationships. Hence a good exercise to do early on in a programme.

See also 1.1 Handshakes (1).

1.36   Can you do this?

What to do

The students form pairs. Each partner thinks of something *physical* he or she can do which the other must try to imitate. This can be something as apparently simple as lifting only one eyebrow or playing a tune on a comb covered with paper; or it may be something seemingly more complex, such as a yoga position. Once the partners have tried to imitate each other, the pairs break up and each person seeks a new partner. Everyone in the class should try to work with at least four different people.

Remarks

Suitable for all levels.

This is a useful ice-breaker, especially with new classes, as it helps to bring strangers together by allowing them to concentrate intently on a physical action (rather than a verbal statement). Little language is needed, since the demonstration is usually quite clear. Towards the end of the exercise, however, there may be *comment, comparison, requests for clarification*, etc.

See also 3.17 What am I doing?, 4.13 Starting from scratch, and other mime exercises.

1.37 Body words

What to do

The class is divided into groups of approximately equal size (seven or eight is a good number). Each group has to find a word with the same number of letters as there are people in the group. Each person then forms one of the letters of the word with his or her body, and the group as a whole presents a visual representation of the entire word for the other groups to interpret.

Remarks

Level: elementary upwards.

Apart from being an enjoyable 'loosening-up' exercise, this is also an activity which provides useful training in *enunciation* and *pronunciation*. It is therefore particularly suitable for elementary or weaker intermediate learners. Useful variants on the pattern described are:

a) The class is divided into small groups of three or four; each group thinks of a word containing at least six letters and forms either the last three or the first three letters of the word. The observers must then try to guess the word from the clues given.

b) Words from course text-books may be introduced: each group is given a slip of paper with a word which is difficult to spell or pronounce; as in a), some of the letters may be omitted.

c) Working in groups of five or six, the students proceed as in *What to do*, but this time they *jumble* the letters, so that the observers must first correctly identify each letter and then work out the word.

Useful as a warming-up exercise for section 5.

See also 7.5 Alphabet poems, 7.6 What's in a name?, section 8 A day's work.

1.38 Becoming a musical instrument

What to do

Students form pairs. Each pair must 'become' a new musical instrument and demonstrate the sound it makes. If they wish, one person can be the player, the other the instrument. Otherwise, both will perform as one instrument, with an imaginary player.

Remarks

Suitable for all levels.

This is a good bridging activity. Language is involved in discussing the shape and sound of the instrument, but the 'musicians'' attention will be focussed on the sound produced. If members of the class seem willing, it is possible to suggest at the end that they perform in concert, playing a well-known melody.

See also 4.16 Making a machine, 3.17 What am I doing? 2.16 Difficulty with large or small objects.

1.39   The sun and the moon

What to do

The whole class stands in the middle of the room. The organizer calls out a pair of words, pointing to one or the other end of the room as he or she says them (e.g. 'Sun!' − left end, 'Moon!' − right end). The members of each of the groups formed in this way then discuss among themselves the reasons for choosing the word.

Some pairs of words which work well are: sun / moon, fire / ice, rose / thorn, red / green, Saturday night / Sunday morning, 11 a.m. / 3 p.m.

Remarks

Level: elementary upwards.

This is a very good ice-breaker. Care should be taken to ensure that the word is chosen without hesitation, on impulse.

One variant is to ask group members from one end of the room to work with a partner from the other end of the room and to try to persuade this person that he or she made the wrong choice of word.

See also section 8 A day's work.

1.40   Not me! It was Jim

What to do

The students sit in circles of about ten. The one who begins accuses one of the others of something, e.g. 'Bill lost the car keys'. Bill (or whoever it is) then replies: 'Who, me? No, it wasn't me who lost them. It was Jim.' Jim (or whoever it is) then repeats the same pattern, accusing someone else. And so on. (It is assumed that the students know each other's names.)

Remarks

Level: elementary upwards.

An effective way of practising patterns without overtly doing a drill. As in 1.45 And I'm a butcher, the language input can be varied to suit the level and character of the class (e.g. 'I'm sorry to have to say this, but I'm pretty sure it was Bill who...' etc.).

See also 5.2 Listen to me!

1.41   Gift of the gab

What to do

The students form pairs. Each places a coin in the palm of the left hand, which is held out towards the partner – no curled fingers!

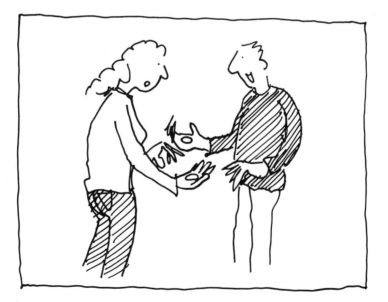

The object of the activity is to engage the partner in conversation and to distract his or her attention so that the coin may be taken. (In order to prevent premature grabbing, no coins may be taken for at least one minute.)

Remarks

Level: elementary to intermediate upwards.

A lighthearted activity which releases a good deal of potentially negative energy. Care must be taken not to let it disintegrate into a free-for-all.

It can be given a tighter structure by handing out slips of paper to everyone on which the topic they are to talk about is written.

See also 5.2 Listen to me!, 5.4 Off the cuff, 5.5 Persuasion, section 8 A day's work.

1.42　My word!

What to do

The students form pairs. Each person has a card with one or more words written on it (e.g. *apple, knife, key, spring, water, cup,* etc.). Partners take it in turn to mime the word to each other, using *hands only.*

Remarks

Some minimal language required.

This is an activity which can be done at several levels of complexity. The examples given are all of simple, concrete nouns. Using verbs, adverbs, or adjectives, or more abstract nouns, can make the discussion of the mime much more fruitful, e.g. *slither* (v), *crumble* (v), *indolently* (adv), *deliberately* (adv), *sly* (adj), *futile* (adj), *breakdown* (n), *strength* (n).

In many of the exercises in this book, the language of discussion generated by the exercise is particularly important. Phrases such as: 'I didn't understand...', 'It wasn't quite clear...' 'I thought you were...', 'But why did you...?', will be needed here, as they will in the more complex exercises of sections 2 and 3.

See also 2.16 Difficulty with large or small objects, 3.1 Exchanging objects, section 8 A day's work.

1.43　Backs

What to do

The students work in pairs. One stands behind the other and traces a simple message on his or her partner's back with a finger. Students are encouraged to exchange interpretative language, e.g. 'Was that an *a*?' 'Please write it again.' 'The first word again, please.' 'Do it a bit more slowly.' etc.

Both partners are given the chance to write.

Remarks

Level: elementary upwards.

The activity allows for physical contact – but in pursuit of information. There is a real straining after meaning, often involving highly vivid visualization. The activity is open to infinite variations. For example, students can be given slips of paper with sentences or words already prepared. These may be used to reinforce structures or vocabulary currently being dealt with.

Alternatively, instead of using words, simple pictures or diagrams may be transmitted, which the receiver then has to redraw. (Here there may be some argument as to the precise shape of the original.)

See also 4.15 Patent pending, 6.8 Shapes and figures, section 8 A day's work.

1.44 What's in a hand?

What to do

The students sit in pairs. Each one holds out the left hand to his or her partner, palm upwards. They are told simply to talk about anything which is suggested to them by their partner's hand.

After five to ten minutes, each pair joins another pair to exchange information about what was discussed.

Remarks

Level: elementary to intermediate upwards.

This deceptively simple activity often gives rise to very interesting discussion. Most often, pairs begin by talking about the size, shape and feel of their hands, ornaments such as rings, etc. But very soon they begin to move on to more personal implications (whether the partner is artistic or practical, etc.).

The comparison of information in groups of four is also highly productive, giving practice in concurring and expressing interest in new information, as well as simple reporting.

See also 1.50 Self-portraits, 3.13 Palmistry, the zodiac and fortune-telling, 6.6 The secret forest, section 8 A day's work.

1.45 And I'm a butcher

What to do

The students sit in circles, facing inwards (about ten to twelve per circle).

One student begins by giving his or her real name and an imaginary profession, e.g. 'I'm Alan, and I'm a butcher'. The student on the right then repeats this information and adds his or her own name and an imaginary profession e.g. 'You're Alan, and you're a butcher. I'm Helen, and I'm a hairdresser'. The next student to the right continues the process, e.g. 'He's Alan, and he's a butcher. You're Helen, and you're a hairdresser. I'm Ann, and I'm a skin-diver'. The process goes on until everyone has added information about himself or herself. The person who began the process then has to repeat the whole series.

Remarks

Level: elementary upwards.

A good exercise to develop careful listening to what others are saying, and to sharpen the memory. (It is best not to exceed twelve people in a circle, otherwise the activity may break down.) It is also good for giving each person a sense of his or her own value – the repetition of one's name by others somehow seems to give satisfaction, particularly to weaker students.

Although here the input is limited to a simple sentence involving a name and a profession, other more complex inputs can be used (perhaps to give practice in structures currently being dealt with), e.g.
– 'I'm Fred, and I like swimming.'
 'I'm Mary, and I like dancing.'
– 'I'm Jim, and I've just come back from Hungary.'
 'I'm Jules, and I'm going to Rovaniemi next week.'
The variations possible are almost limitless.

See also 2.15 I say, you said, he said, 3.18 The hotel receptionist.

1.46 The seat on my left is free

What to do

The students sit in circles (about ten per circle) with one chair left empty. It is assumed that they all know each other's names.

The person with an empty seat on the left says: 'The seat on my left is free, and I'd like (Maureen) to sit next to me.' Maureen (or who-ever it is) then moves to the vacant seat, leaving her own place vacant. The person who now has the vacant seat on the left repeats the pro-cess, and so on.

Remarks

Level: elementary upwards.

A fun activity, which gets the students accustomed to using their names with familiarity, and which gives plenty of opportunity for mixing.

See also 1.64 I've got my eye on you!, 2.5 Spot the change.

1.47 Like me? Like you? Like who?

What to do

The class is divided into pairs. Both partners write down on a slip of paper three ways in which they think they are *different* from their partner, and three ways in which they think they are the *same* as or *similar* to their partner. Partners then exchange papers and use them as a basis for discussion.

Remarks

Level: elementary upwards.

This obviously works better in classes which already have a certain experience of working together.

It gives opportunities for unexpected revelations to be made, and these often form the basis of quite deep conversations.

It may be worth putting pairs together to form fours, but this must be at the discretion of the organizer.

See also 1.50 Self-portraits, 2.11 This is me, 2.12 clues.

1.48 Let me tell you something about X

What to do

All the students walk about the room, mixing freely. When the word is given, everyone finds out *one* piece of personal information from the person nearest to him or her, and then moves on to another per-son to whom this information is passed on. The process goes on con-tinuously until the organizer calls a halt.

Remarks

Level: elementary upwards.

A good way of mixing people up initially and getting them to exchange a little personal information. Also good for practice in the language of reporting, e.g. 'Brenda told me she likes doughnuts', 'Keith said he was tired', etc.

Care must be taken to stop people from getting into long conversations, and to keep them on the move.

If there is time, everyone should sit down for a feedback session, when they try to remember what they have learned about each other.

See also 1.56 and 1.57 Childhood memories (1 and 2), 4.7 It means a lot to me.

1.49 Interviews (1)

What to do

Everyone is given several copies of the questionnaire below. They are told that in the space of fifteen minutes they have to gather the information required by interviewing as many people in the room as possible.

Questionnaire

First name .... Surname ....

Address .... Home telephone no. ....

.... Children? (If so—names) ....

Married/single ....

Occupation .... Business telephone no. ....

Favourite spare-time occupation ....

Remarks

Level: elementary to intermediate upwards.

A good exercise for any new group.

Clearly, anyone who agrees to be interviewed has the right to interview in turn.

Besides giving the opportunity to exchange information, this exercise also offers practice in various ways of asking for information, e.g. 'Would you mind telling me...?' 'I wonder if I could ask...?' 'Could you tell me...?' etc. Later, the students could be asked to devise their own questionnaires to obtain different information.

See also 6.3 Our choice, 6.7 Alibi, 3.12 Interviews (2), 3.23 Talk of the Devil.

1.50 Self-portraits

What to do

All the students draw self-portraits in which they exaggerate the feature they think most characterizes them (e.g. long eyelashes, big beard, shaggy hair, wide nostrils, etc.). No one shows his or her self-portrait to anyone else. The class is then divided into two *equal* groups which go to opposite sides of the room. The portraits are folded, collected and exchanged between the groups (i.e. group A gets the portraits from group B, and vice versa). They are then distributed among the members of each group. It is now the task of each student to identify the person who drew the portrait and to discuss it with him or her, and with others.

Remarks

Level: elementary upwards.

Many people will object that they cannot draw. They should be gently persuaded that even a small effort will be acceptable (and that they are not alone in being unable to draw!).

The discussion is usually very lively and reveals a good deal of sympathy for those who may have been too hard on their own personal appearance.

It is often worth pinning up the results for a few days on the display board. This helps to develop a sense of solidarity within the class, and fosters the emergence of 'characters'.

See also 1.67 Portraits (1), 2.12 Clues, 3.20 Becoming a picture.

1.51 Something in common (1)

What to do

Each person is asked to note down four things, such as the following:
− a *superstition* (in which you either believe or do not believe);
− an apparatus/*machine*/mechanical device that annoys you;
− anything that evokes a powerful *childhood memory* (e.g. a song, a street name);
− *tics* or habits that irritate you in others.

This should take not more than two or three minutes. Now, each person should go round comparing his or her list with those of the others in the class. Everyone should try to speak to everyone else, while remembering who had similar responses to the four items. Those with similar responses should discuss the points they have in common and the points on which they differ.

If the exercise is to be used only for warming up, it can be stopped after the discussion. There is, however, an interesting extension which is well worth trying if time permits. It is described in full in 4.6 Something in common (2).

Remarks

Level: elementary to intermediate upwards.

It is always intriguing to discover that one shares likes or dislikes with someone else. 'Having something in common' (even if it is negative) is a useful basis for any work with a partner. In this exercise, one could use almost any four elements (e.g. a colour, a time of day, a type of landscape, an animal), provided they were sufficiently disparate. The four given above are merely examples. In the early stage of the exercise, students should be encouraged to *expand* on the four items when discussing and comparing.

See also 2.11 This is me, 4.6 Something in common (2).

1.52 Leading the blind

What to do

The students are divided into two equal groups. Each group forms pairs. The centre of the room is filled with 'obstacles' (e.g. chairs), with passages left in between. One member of each pair from group A goes to the opposite end of the room. The remaining partners are then blindfolded (or close their eyes). The 'guides' then give directives to their partners to enable them to walk through the obstacles without touching them. Anyone touching an obstacle is eliminated. Then group B does the same.

Remarks

Level: elementary upwards.

An exercise developing trust between partners, precision in the language of instructions and careful listening (in natural conditions – with background noise!).

See also 1.23 Blind, 2.18 Lost memory, 5.2 Listen to me!

1.53 Group dream

What to do

The students lie (or sit) with eyes closed, in silence. Anyone may initiate a dream (which may be the beginning of a real dream they have had, or simply an image which has just come into their mind). Others may join in at any time to add details or to move the action along. Gradually, a composite group dream emerges.

Remarks

Level: elementary upwards.

Obviously, this requires a class with a good deal of experience in working together, and confidence in using the language.

Like 1.54 Directed group fantasies, this can be developed into writing, or a dramatization of the dream.

See also 2.10 Listening with eyes closed, 3.30 Dream themes.

1.54 Directed group fantasies

What to do

Students lie (or sit) with eyes closed. The organizer then begins to relate a highly visual, atmospheric story, in a calm slow voice. For example:

It is just a small country railway station, with a ticket collector fast asleep under his newspaper, a fly buzzing on the window, roses and hollyhocks growing sweet in the flower-beds. You walk out into the midday sun. There is no village to be seen, only a long, winding, dusty road disappearing into a wood. Time seems to have stopped. You walk slowly up the road and into the delicious cool of the shade. In the distance, the road seems to come to an end with a pair of high wrought-iron gates. As you come nearer, you see there are two large stone lions on each side of the gate – the kind you vaguely remember seeing in photographs of the East. Through the gate you can make out a gate-house, with massive windowless walls and only one low archway. The walls are painted dark blood-red, and under the arch it is black. There is a small gate to the side of the larger gates. You go through it, and walk towards the menace of the gate-house, which you now notice has a Chinese curving roof. As you walk into the pitch darkness of the arch, your blood freezes...

The speaker goes on up to a point where he or she feels the class can take over, and then stops. Any student can take the story a stage further by adding one or more sentences.

Remarks

Level: elementary to intermediate upwards.

It is important to give the students long enough to get into the story before leaving it to them. And not to hurry them, as it usually takes a minute or two before anyone speaks. Do not worry about this silence – it is productive silence. And do not let the activity go on for too long. You will soon tell if it starts to flag. Clearly, the dream can be followed up by writing or dramatization.

See also 7.4 Starters.

1.55 Hunter and hunted

What to do

The students are divided into two groups of equal numbers. Those in the one group imagine they are predators or hunters, those in the other group that they are animals which are usually hunted. The animals can be fish or insects as well as the more common beasts of prey.

Each person then becomes the animal he or she has chosen. The predators seek their prey. But, before devouring their prey, they must identify it. This means that, for instance, the shark cannot attack the hedgehog, and the lion cannot attack the fly. In cases of doubt, e.g. lion vs. hedgehog, the two animals discuss whether the predator has the right to attack his or her prey. (Doubtful cases are argued out before the 'animal court'.)

Remarks

Level: elementary upwards.

This is a warming-up exercise, but, because it involves discussion, it may go beyond the usual limits of warming-up exercises. The animals in the 'hunted' group should be reminded that they have the right to use their natural techniques of self-protection (poison, loss of a limb e.g. the lizard's tail, etc.).

It is specifically intended as a warming-up exercise for 4.21.

1.56 Childhood memories (1)

What to do

Each person writes down a single word which represents a childhood memory. It is necessary for the students to be reminded that this word need be meaningful only to themselves personally. It might be a colour (e.g. *brown, violet*); it might be a smell (e.g. *cabbage, floor-polish*); it might be the name of a place, a person, or a song; it might be an object (e.g. *ashtray, vase*); it might be a date, even a day. Abstract words, such as *happiness, hope, courage*, should be avoided.

The slips of paper are then collected and redistributed at random. Each person now tries to find who wrote the word on his or her slip of paper. (He or she should *say* the word aloud, not show the slip of paper.) When the right person is found, he or she should explain what memory was associated with the word. In turn, the other person should say what word he or she had written down and what memory it was associated with.

Remarks

Level: elementary to intermediate upwards.

If a class is going to work together regularly, it is important that the members should see each other as people, not just members of a class. This does not mean that we want to hear their life story or to learn their personal secrets. Nobody should be expected to reveal what he or she does not want. Childhood memories, of course, are often painful. This is why we ask the students to write down the word on paper. If they have memories they prefer to suppress, they will not write down anything that might recall them. Also, the act of writing down the word gives added precision to the memory. For each memory will involve many different facets, and the writing will help to make clear which of these is the most important.

It is best to use this activity only after the class has been working together for some time.

See also 4.7 It means a lot to me, 7.9 Amnesty.

1.57 Childhood memories (2)

What to do

The students lie (or sit) with eyes closed. They are asked to think about a very vivid childhood memory: to remember it, not just in general, but in every smallest particular – the colours, smells, textures and shapes, the people involved and their associations, what was in the background, etc. Enough time must be allowed (five to ten minutes) for the memory to be vividly recalled.

Students then exchange memories by talking to each other in pairs.

Remarks

Level: intermediate upwards.

This is an extension of the previous exercise, and is a very powerful activity which can be developed in many directions: into group discussion, into dramatization of incidents, into writing (see the article by Anne Péchou, 'The Magic Carpet', in *English Teaching Forum*, vol. XIX, no. 2, 1981).

An alternative stimulus is to ask students to recall a recent vivid dream.

See also 4.21 Zoo story, 4.22 Dream home.

1.58 Down under

What to do

Each person is asked to think of a well-known figure from history (fictional characters are also allowed) and imagine they are that person. Alternatively the names of such personalities are written on cards and handed to the students. The advantage of preparing the names in advance is that it makes it possible to establish connections between the different figures, e.g. Caesar–Cleopatra, Leonardo–Mona Lisa, Pickwick–Dickens, Tristan–Isolde, etc.

These characters are all in hell (or heaven or purgatory, if you prefer!). Naturally, they do not recognize each other. Each person moves round the room, talking to the others. The idea is to establish contact through *indirect* questioning, i.e. one question cannot be asked: 'Who are you?' They should try to find out as much as possible about each other, without ever saying explicitly *who* they are. After ten to fifteen minutes, a round-up session is held. Students relate who they think they were talking to, but without indicating the characters in person, e.g. 'I spoke to Cleopatra about... and to Karl Marx about...'. After this, any misunderstandings are cleared up.

Remarks

Level: intermediate upwards.

This was originally developed as a way of incorporating latecomers into a group. As each person came into the room, he or she was told simply to imagine that he or she was a well-known person, who was in hell, and who had to make contact with the others there without trying directly to find out who they were. The exercise is a good test in listening and reacting to what is said. If the alternative (above) is used, no difference need be made between the sexes. Men can take women's characters, and women men's, provided that everyone knows this may happen.

See also 3.7 Mixed sets, 2.12 Clues, 3.12 Interviews, 7.6 What's in a name?

GROUP-FORMATION EXERCISES

1.59   Strings

What to do

The organizer takes a number of lengths of string (half as many as there are people in the class), holding the bundle so that the ends come out on either side of the hand, like this:

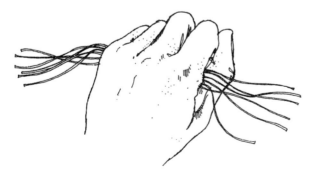

Each student then takes hold of one of the ends. The organizer releases the bundle, and the students are in pairs. The exercise can be repeated if groups of four are needed.

Remarks

Suitable for all levels.

Forming groups is not always as easy as it sounds. Much time can be wasted if students hunt around for the people they would *like* to work with. If one plans to use drama techniques regularly, it is essential that everyone in the class should be willing to work with everyone else. As they grow to know each other, the students will come to realize that personal antipathies *can* be overcome, and that often the most exciting work arises from cooperation with a seemingly 'hostile' partner or group. In the early stages, therefore, it is important to have a few 'democratic' group-forming techniques up one's sleeve.

1.60 Atom 3!

What to do

The students move freely about the room to music (lively music, such as Stravinsky's 'Rite of Spring', African drum music, South American folk music, or even Strauss waltzes, is most suitable). The organizer stops the music unexpectedly, and calls out: 'Atom 3!' (or 2 or 7 or 11, but never a number larger than the actual size of the class), and the students join together with those nearest to them to form the requisite number.

After this has been repeated several times, the organizer calls out the number he or she requires for the group activity to follow (e.g. 'Atom 4'). Groups of four are then ready-made.

Remarks

Suitable for all levels.

Strictly speaking, the exercise should be called 'Molecule 3!', – but 'Atom 3!' is easier to shout!

See also 1.28 Slow motion, 2.2 Freeze!, 4.9 Statues.

1.61 Mix

What to do

The students move freely about the room (the use of music is optional). When the word is given, each person takes the hand of the person next to him or her. The pairs then move hand-in-hand together. When next the word is given, each pair joins hands with the nearest other pair. This produces groups of four.

Remarks

Suitable for all levels.

1.62   Find your group

What to do

Material needed: cards – sufficient for every member of the class to have one. Below is an example of a simple set for eight people who need to be divided into groups of four.

1	Me	Him	**2**	Me	Her
Name	Alan	Jim	*Name*	Jim	May
Age	43	19	*Age*	19	39
	Two sons. Lives in Birmingham. Works in car factory.	One brother – Ray. Lives in Birmingham. Out of work. Father works in car-factory.		One brother – Ray. Lives in Birmingham. Out of work. Father works in car factory.	Two sons. Husband works in car-factory.
3	Me	Him	**4**	Me	Him
Name	May	Ray	*Name*	Ray	Alan
Age	39	16	*Age*	16	43
	Two sons. Husband works in car factory.	At school. Likes climbing.		At school. Likes climbing.	Two sons. Lives in Birmingham. Works in car-factory.

The next set of eight cards is the same, except in *one* particular, e.g. Alan, 43, *three daughters*; Ray, 16, *unemployed*... Thus it is important that everyone should ask for *all* information on the other person's card.

Each person identifies with the *me* on his or her card, and goes looking for the *him* or *her*. This involves asking questions of the other people in the class. It is not sufficient to ask one or two questions only, since the information is so designed that there are two *hims* and *hers* around with very similar characteristics. The activity continues until the groups of four are formed.

Remarks

Level: elementary upwards.

The students should be encouraged to memorize the information on their cards, as this will oblige them to speak instead of merely showing each other their cards. As considerable preparation is required here, the group-formation exercise could be profitably extended into a full activity.

See also 3.6 Split exchanges, 3.12 Interviews (2).

1.63 Identikit

What to do

Material needed: a set of pictures cut from magazines. The number of pictures should correspond to the number of groups to be formed. Each picture should then be cut into the number of pieces corresponding to the number of people required in each group (e.g. if six groups of four are required, cut each of the six pictures into four).

The pieces of all pictures are mixed up, and the students take one piece each at random. They then circulate, and by *questions only* (no showing of pictures) try to find the other members of 'their' picture. The groups are then formed. (A possible variation is to distribute extracts from the same poem, advertisement, paragraph, etc.)

Remarks

Level: elementary upwards.

This exercise, like the previous four, depends on the random principle. No choice is involved. For many activities this is desirable, since it stops the better students from clubbing together in immutable groups to the detriment of the weaker or shyer members.

See also 3.6 Split exchanges, 6.5 Split cartoons, 6.8 Shapes and figures.

1.64 I've got my eye on you!

What to do

The students stand in two lines facing each other – an equal number in each line. To begin with, everyone in each line should look very carefully at every person in the opposite line, but not dwelling too long on any one person.

Then each person tries to catch the eye of a person in the opposite line. When a pair of eyes 'agrees' on a partnership, the partners separate off. The pairs then line up opposite each other and try to catch the 'eye' of a pair in the opposite line. Thus groups of four are formed.

Remarks

Suitable for all levels.

1.65 I know what I like

What to do

Each student writes on a slip of paper three things he or she likes very much, and three things he or she dislikes very much. The students then circulate freely trying to find a partner who shares as many likes and dislikes as possible. The pairs then go in search of others who may share the same tastes. This may lead to groups of non-uniform size, but for some activities this does not matter. It is important that the students talk to each other and do not simply show each other their slips of paper.

Remarks

Level: elementary upwards.

One might be tempted to ask: 'Why bother with the writing at all, if it is not to be used?' Not only in this exercise, but in many others, students will be asked to write and then disregard what they have written (or memorize it). The reason is that writing something down gives it a finality: it is there, and cannot be changed. In discussion, it is easy to be influenced by what one's partner says, easy to retract or alter one's own ideas. It is to avoid this happening that we occasionally suggest writing, without any evident reason for doing so.

See also 4.6 Something in common (2), 4.7 It means a lot to me.

1.66   Same/different

What to do

Each student chooses two other people in the class – without telling them, of course – and notes down on a slip of paper two ways in which they are similar to him or her, and two ways in which they are different. The students then circulate, talking to the people they have chosen about their similarities and differences. Since the same three people do not usually choose each other, this leads to the formation of groups of at least five.

Remarks

Level: elementary upwards.

See also 1.50 Self-portraits, 1.51 and 4.6 Something in common (1 and 2).

1.67   Portraits (1)

What to do

Each student decides on another person in the room he or she would like to work with. He or she draws on a piece of paper as accurate a picture as possible of that person. The students circulate, trying to identify themselves. Once again, as the same two people do not usually choose each other, this leads to considerable discussion before the groups are finally formed.

Remarks

Level: elementary upwards.

   The previous three exercises are ones which allow students some degree of choice as to whom they work with. This may be desirable for some types of activities. It is up to the organizer to decide whether random groups or groups formed on the basis of personal affiliation are to be preferred. A time limit of approximately ten minutes will need to be set for these activities.

See also 2.4 Back-to-back, 2.11 This is me.

2 Observation

2.1 Metronome mimes

What to do

a) One person should be asked to beat out a slow, regular rhythm, like that of a metronome.

   The class is divided into pairs. The people in each pair sit side-by-side. A simple, everyday action is suggested, e.g. cutting bread, drinking. This action must be performed in 'clockwork' movement, so that what would normally be a fluid action is broken up into distinct stages. Each member of the pair should try to keep pace with his or her partner.

b) The students are still in pairs, but face to face. Each pair decides on its own action. All actions are performed to the same rhythm.

c) Again in pairs: one is the mirror, the other the 'actor'. In the first stage, only the head and arms are used. A simple action is performed, e.g. combing hair, putting on eyeshadow. The mirror should imitate this action as accurately as possible. It is, therefore, best to suggest that the actions be performed in *slow motion*.

   In the second stage, a full-length mirror is used. Each pair should decide where their mirror is (in a lift, on a staircase, etc.) and choose a situation to mime. This may be an action involving several sequences, e.g. dropping a bag and picking up the contents. They should try to synchronize their movements as closely as possible. When they are ready, they perform their 'mirror sequence' for another pair, who will try to interpret each stage of the action.

Remarks

Level: elementary upwards.

   This is an exercise in physical concentration. Language is expected only in the last stage. (There will, however, be language work in the preparation.)

See also 1.3 Mirror hands, 2.6 What am I holding?, 4.16 Making a machine.

2.2   Freeze!

What to do

Material needed: music, preferably with a varied rhythm (e.g. Stravinsky's 'Fire-bird'). The tape or record is played to the whole class. Everyone moves to the music in whatever way he or she likes. When the music stops, everyone freezes. All positions must be held. Each person notes his or her posture at the moment of freezing, and his or her position relative to those closest.

Variant 1: The music now continues and everyone carries on moving. When the music stops, all must return to their *original* positions, i.e. as they were at the end of the first piece. Disagreements should be settled by (brief) discussion.

Variant 2: No more music is played. Everyone is told to note his or her position very carefully (but without making any notes). The exercise is now abandoned until the end of the session, and other activities are performed. At the end of the morning or afternoon, the same music is played again, and stopped at the same point. Everyone freezes, then moves to take up the position he or she had when the music was first played several hours earlier.

Remarks

Suitable for all levels.

If videotape is available, this could be used as a means of checking the original positions. Without videotape, however, the exercise may be even more linguistically enriching, since there is no final arbiter but the collective memory.

See also 1.28 Slow motion, 1.60 Atom 3!, 2.5 Spot the change, 3.19 Portraits (2), 4.9 Statues, section 8 A day's work.

2.3   Observation of the room

What to do

All the furniture should be moved out of the way. The students are then asked to walk round the room and 'have a good look at it' for not more than about two minutes. They are then suddenly told to close their eyes.

The organizer now asks five or six simple questions, such as: 'How many doors/lights are there?' 'What colour are the curtains?' 'Are any of the windows open?' 'Is anything written on the board?' etc. The students should listen to these questions without trying to answer them aloud. When the word is given, they open their eyes and check their impressions with the person standing next to them.

Usually they will spontaneously tell each other what they remembered correctly and what they got wrong, but it may at times be necessary to move round reminding them of the questions.

Remarks

Level: elementary upwards.

This can, of course, be used simply as a warming-up exercise. But it has a further specific function: to reveal how unexpectedly interesting familiar objects become once they can no longer be seen (or heard, or touched). The closer the observation, the greater will be the subsequent interest. Many of the exercises in this book demand attention to detail; practice in observation is therefore essential.

See also 2.8 Familiar scenes, 2.14 If I remember rightly..., 2.17 Kim's game.

2.4 **Back-to-back**

What to do

The students are asked to walk round the room looking at each other and trying to notice as many details of appearance as possible. (Classes over twenty could be split into two.)

After two or three minutes, they are told to stop and to stand back-to-back with the person nearest. The partners now take it in turns to describe each other's appearance without turning round. Partner B (who is being described) should neither confirm nor refute what partner A says. He or she may, however, press for a more accurate description, e.g.

    A: You're wearing blue.
    B: Dark blue or light blue?
or
    A: You're wearing glasses.
    B: With metal or plastic rims?

When ready, the partners turn round and compare their descriptions with 'the truth'.

A variant of the exercise is to begin with the instructions for 2.3 Observation of the room, but with the students themselves asking the questions. One person in each pair asks questions about the room;

the other answers with eyes closed. When they have finished they discuss the answers together. This means that the questioner must *attend carefully* to the replies. The second time round, the former questioner has eyes closed, but instead of answering questions about the room he or she must give a description of his or her partner's appearance. This usually comes as a surprise, and the students realize (too late) that in concentrating on what was around them they had failed to observe what was right before them!

Remarks

Level: elementary upwards.

By a simple twist, a familiar situation is turned into an unfamiliar one. If the partners had simply been asked to describe each other face-to-face, boredom would rapidly have set in. The 'trick' of working with eyes closed helps to create a tension, which is sustained until the moment of 'revelation' when the eyes are opened. This release of tension also releases the tongue. The students spontaneously comment on what they had said earlier. Such immediacy of reaction is extremely difficult to achieve convincingly in other ways, e.g. through dialogue imitation.

The exercise is something of a shock tactic, and can therefore not be used in this form more than two or three times a year. Variants, however, are easy to devise, e.g. by extending the observation beyond the room itself, to things seen on other occasions, to the street outside or to the town itself.

See also 2.17 Kim's game, and exercises involving the use of pictures (e.g. 3.20 Becoming a picture, 3.21 Bringing a picture to life, 3.22 Picture sets).

2.5 Spot the change

What to do

Groups of eight to ten students face each other in lines. They look carefully at *where* the members of the opposite team are standing and at *what* they are wearing. After three or four minutes, the groups go to different corners of the room and try to remember together the full details of the opposing team. While they are doing this, they discreetly exchange articles of clothing or alter details of their appearance (e.g. letting down their hair – literally, of course!).

After five to eight minutes, the teams come back to face each other, but standing in a different order. The members of the first team take it in turn to say one thing that has changed in the opposite team. They continue until they run out of things to say. It is then the turn of the opposing team to do the same. (The team which spots the greatest number of changes is the winner.)

A variant of this exercise can be done with the groups (of five to seven) standing in circles. The organizer taps one person in each circle on the shoulder: with eyes closed, this person attempts to describe anyone in the circle as accurately as possible. The second time round, two or three people in the group can be made to change positions. The person who was tapped on the shoulder then opens eyes and describes the changes. A third time round, *everyone* in the circle closes eyes; two or three people in each circle are tapped on the shoulder. They leave the room, and while they are away exchange articles of clothing. Those remaining in the room discuss among themselves the appearance of those missing. When the missing persons return, the members of their groups try to spot the changes.

Remarks

Level: elementary upwards.

This is also a good exercise for warming up and for group formation. It has two further advantages in being both enjoyable and linguistically undemanding (mostly language of identification – 'You had a...', 'You were wearing a...'; and, checking up – 'Weren't you wearing...?' 'Didn't you have...?').

See also 2.14 If I remember rightly...

2.6   What am I holding?

What to do

The class is divided into groups of five or six. The groups stand in a circle, each person facing inwards, with hands held cupped behind back. The organizer then slips a small object, e.g. a safety-pin, a coin, or a matchbox, into the hands of *one* member of each group. This person can feel the object, of course, but cannot see it.

The group's task is to discover by questioning what the object is.

Remarks

Level: elementary upwards.

Before using this exercise, it is worth giving a demonstration to the class as a whole. A volunteer stands facing the class, with hands behind back: a small object is slipped into his or her hands, and he or she answers the class's questions. This enables the class to discover together what kind of questions work best.

In this exercise, the questioners have nothing, initially, to guide them. They rely exclusively, therefore, on what can be learnt from their questions. In order to avoid loose guesses ('Is it a drawing pin?') and vague questions ('Is it big?' 'Is it nice?'), the students should be encouraged to use strategies which will progressively eliminate the possibilities, e.g. 'Is it hard?' 'Is it made of metal?' 'Can it be bent?' 'Is it precious?'

See also 3.4 What am I wearing?, 3.17 What am I doing?

2.7 My potato

What to do

Any common fruit or vegetable can be used. Potatoes, apples, tomatoes, carrots, bananas, or nuts are particularly suitable. The class is divided into groups of six to nine (never less than six). Each group is given a pile of potatoes (or apples or tomatoes etc.). There should be at least four more potatoes than there are people in the group. Each person takes out a potato from the pile on the floor and examines it carefully. After about two minutes, the potatoes are returned to the pile, and the pile is mixed. Once it has been mixed, each person must find his or her *own* potato. Those who have no difficulty in finding their potato should turn to the person next to them and exchange potatoes. Each then tries to discover what his or her partner considered to be the characteristic features of his or her potato. Those who do not find their potatoes will have to hunt around!

Remarks

Level: elementary upwards.

This exercise is not as absurd as it may seem. Many of the exercises in this book rely on accuracy of observation (particularly the mime exercises and those in which pictures are used). Here we are developing the ability to recognize *minimal differences*.

See also 4.4 Potato figures, 4.5 Cork, stone and wood.

2.8 Familiar scenes

What to do

The students begin by working in pairs. Each pair draws up a short list (not more than ten items) of easily observed features of the town which they are in. These would include, e.g.
- the exact colour of post-boxes and any words that appear on the boxes;
- the precise shape of the lamp-posts in the main street;
- the shape/design of any common signs (e.g. the sign for a pharmacy, a well-known chain-store/supermarket); the colour of bus/tram/metro tickets;
- the exact position and number of seats in buses/trams;
- any prominent statues or figures on public buildings;
- the wording of the notice inside the lift in the building where they are working, etc.

Eight to ten minutes can be allowed for preparation of questions. The pairs then break up. Each person goes round the room asking as many people as possible questions about the features listed. Any differences in the answers should be noted. Each person then goes back to his or her first partner to compare notes. If the group is not too large, the exercise can end with each pair being asked to give *two* examples of questions which nobody answered correctly, or which gave rise to great disagreement.

Remarks

Level: elementary upwards.

Clearly, this can be done only if all the students are reasonably familiar with the town or city. The exercise should be done 'cold' the first time. This is to ensure that the discussion will be based entirely on *remembered* details. It is, in a sense, an exercise in undirected observation. Students should be reminded to demand as much accuracy as possible in the answers to their questions (especially in talking of colours). The exercise can then be done on another occasion, this time with advance warning. The students would then be asked to prepare their lists *on site* a day or two before.

See also 2.14 If I remember rightly..., 6.7 Alibi.

2.9 Taste, touch, smell

What to do

The class is divided into groups of four or five. Each group decides on something to eat or drink, and works out a way of miming the appropriate actions. The groups then dissolve, and each person finds someone from another group with whom to exchange mimes. Each should try to discover what the other has in mind, and comment critically on what was shown. (Before beginning, the students may need to be reminded of some of the basic language of criticism and approval.)

The same can now be done with the senses of touch and smell. This time, however, the students should think not only of something they might be touching or smelling (e.g. sticky tape, a hot iron, perfumes in a shop, frying onions), but also of *who* they are and *why* they happen to be where they are. It is therefore preferable this time that they develop their ideas in pairs – each partner helping and criticizing the other – and then break up to find different partners with whom to exchange mimes.

Remarks

Level: elementary upwards.

This is a simple exercise in which everyone can take part without difficulty. The actions are familiar, and the choice of ideas is left to the students: this ensures that they will not be stretched beyond their limits. *Note:* it is important *not* to place any stress on the mime itself, i.e. not to give 'practice in mime' beforehand, as this will almost certainly have the counter-effect of making the students self-conscious.

See also 3.17 What am I doing?, 3.18 The hotel receptionist.

2.10 Listening with eyes closed

What to do

The students are asked to close their eyes and to listen intently to all sounds, inside and outside the room. After a couple of minutes, they open their eyes and jot down everything they heard.

If there are more than twenty in the class, groups of five or six should be formed for the next stage.

Each person now mentions one sound on his or her list, but without commenting on it. After each person in the group has mentioned a sound, the details are added, e.g. the strength of the sound, where it came from, what it was caused by. First to speak is the person on whose list the sound appeared; the others in the group qualify his or her remarks with their own comments. If a group cannot agree on a particular sound it can later call in other groups for a second or third opinion.

Remarks

Level: elementary upwards.

Again, the purpose is to present the familiar in an unfamiliar way. The important difference here, however, is that while visual details *can* be checked, this is not always possible with sounds. As a result, other kinds of language will now be needed, e.g. expressions of conviction ('I'm sure it wasn't a bird!'), doubt ('It didn't sound like a siren to me'), disagreement ('But it was different each time!'). Notice, too, that common knowledge will be used, rightly or wrongly, to back up statements, e.g. 'It couldn't have been a car turning left, because this is a one-way street.'

See also 2.17 Kim's game, 2.14 If I remember rightly...

2.11 This is me

What to do

Each student writes down on a slip of paper a sentence which will serve to identify him or her. The slips of paper are then folded, mixed up and redistributed. Students then go round asking questions based on what is on their slip of paper, in order to find the person described.

Remarks

Level: elementary upwards.

This can be made more highly structured by giving guidelines, e.g. 'Write five sentences on: your appearance, your character, what you like doing best, who your best friend is, what your favourite food is. You have five minutes.'

This can be used as a basis for group formation, but it usually takes longer than one would normally wish to spend simply on setting up groups.

Variations are easily introduced. For example, students can be asked to write down three early childhood memories, or three things they do well, etc. The important thing is to have something personal on the slip of paper to serve as a jumping-off point for talking.

See also 1.36 Can you do this?, 1.56 and 1.57 Childhood memories (1 and 2), 1.51 and 4.6 Something in common (1 and 2).

2.12 Clues

What to do

Each student writes down a list of ten items associated with himself or herself – items which a detective would find in his or her room if he or she was kidnapped. These things would give clues to the detective about the kind of person he or she was.

The slips of paper are then mixed up and redistributed. Working in pairs, the students discuss the two lists of items they share, and try to identify the two people concerned. After this discussion phase, each person interviews anyone he or she thinks may correspond with the details on his or her slip of paper.

Remarks

Level: intermediate upwards.

The pooling of information in pairs before interviewing is an important part of the activity, and should not be skated over.

The activity gives good opportunities for observation, speculation, and learning about other people in the group.

See also 1.50 Self-portraits, 1.51 and 4.6 Something in common (1 and 2), 2.17 Kim's game, 3.12 Interviews (2), 3.25 Detective work.

2.13 From my album

What to do

The students are asked to bring to class two photographs of special interest to themselves.

Working in pairs, the students show each other their photographs. Each explains why the photograph is of particular interest to himself or herself; the partner should feel free to ask further questions about the background to the photographs, striking details, etc. After five minutes, everyone changes partners, and a new discussion begins.

When the second discussion is finished, each student places *one* of his or her photographs in a pile, and each selects *one* that he or she has not yet seen. The task is now to find the owner of the photograph, not by showing the photograph but by *describing* it. In this case, the discussions are briefer. The photographs are then returned to the pile, and each student links up with his or her *original* partner.

Now, without showing their photograph (the one that was not put into the pile), the partners recreate in as much detail as possible the photograph they saw at the beginning of the exercise.

Remarks

Level: intermediate upwards.

This is an exercise in *attentiveness*: what the eye sees is reinforced by what the ear hears. A similar technique is used in several of the exercises with pictures, the difference being that here the students have a *personal* interest in the photographs. If time allows, each pair could be asked to join up with another. As a group of four they should invent a *plausible* story connecting the four photographs. All the original facts must be retained, but additional (fictional) information may be added for the sake of the story.

See also 1.51 and 4.6 Something in common (1 and 2), 2.14 If I remember rightly...

2.14 If I remember rightly...

What to do

Material needed: a set of pictures with strong focal points of interest (see examples below). There should be enough pictures for every person in the class to have one.

Working in groups of four, the students study all the pictures in their group. They should feel free to comment on the pictures to each other, but should not attempt to 'interpret' them. The only instruction they are given at this stage is to 'observe the details carefully'.

After five minutes, all groups turn their pictures face down. Each group – with all four members working together – now writes down as many details of each picture as can be remembered. Any disagreements over points of detail should also be noted. The observations should be as accurate as possible, e.g. if two people are standing together, the note should indicate not simply that A is taller than B, but that B's head comes up to A's shoulder, or is level with A's ear. After five minutes, the groups are given two minutes only to check their lists against the pictures.

Each group now chooses another group to work with. They exchange their sets of pictures: group A now has group B's pictures, and vice versa. The members of group B now describe the pictures they have just given to group A; group A questions them on points of detail ('You say there were bottles on the doorstep – how many? Were they all on the same step?' etc.). When this is finished, group A then describes its pictures to group B. Finally, both groups compare what was said with the lists they wrote earlier.

Remarks

Level: intermediate to advanced.

Here we are extending the powers of observation developed in earlier exercises, such as 2.3 Observation of the room.

In the first stage, i.e. looking at the pictures, there will be relatively little language, as attention is concentrated on observing details. In the second stage, i.e. compiling the list, there will be a tendency for everyone to speak at once. It is up to each group to find its own way of overcoming this (the ability to get one's word in against vociferous competition is a skill worth developing), but it may be necessary to remind the more unruly groups that it is *essential* to establish a written list of the group's comments. They should also be reminded that points of disagreement are to be noted. When, later, the group comes to be examined on the pictures, the 'truth' will be all the more interesting on account of this internal opposition. Note that with advanced groups or groups familiar with this kind of work, no time should be allowed for checking the list quickly against the pictures; they should move straight on to working with another group. The two minutes' quick check is intended only for the weaker or more reticent groups.

In the third stage, there may well be a shift from the past tense – mainly used when compiling the list – to the present tense. This is because when the group is being questioned on the pictures, they once again become a *present* reality. There will also be a fair amount of *repetition* and *reformulation*, especially if the questions of the other group reveal divergences of opinion, or if group B's answers are not felt to be sufficiently accurate, e.g.

A: What's the man doing?
B: Standing.
A: On both legs?
B: Oh, no, only on one. In fact, he's leaning against the wall.

So, throughout the activity various different language tactics will be used: first, identification and comment; then persuasion, polite disagreement, challenging, checking up, and reformulation; and finally repetition and further reformulation.

See also 2.3 Observation of the room, 2.10 Listening with eyes closed, 2.17 Kim's game, 7.9 Amnesty.

2.15   I say, you said, he said

What to do

The students work in groups of three. One person (A) tells about an incident in his or her life (a recent event, or a particularly interesting memory). The second person (B) listens carefully, taking notes if necessary. When A has finished, B has to retell the story as accurately as possible. When B has finished, it is the turn of C to correct any errors of fact or omissions which B may have made. Each person (A, B, and C) has a turn in each role.

Remarks

Level: advanced.
   The stories should clearly not be too long. The activity encourages careful listening and gives the opportunity for repetition and correction within an interesting framework.

See also 1.56 and 1.57 Childhood memories (1 and 2), 1.51 and 4.6 Something in common (1 and 2), 3.22 Picture sets.

2.16   Difficulty with large or small objects

What to do

The class is divided into groups of four or five. Each group decides on a number of small objects, such as a needle, a key, a shoelace, a coin.
   Either individually or as a group, the students work out brief sketches showing the difficulties they might have with such objects, e.g. threading a needle while sitting in a train; tying a shoelace with frostbitten fingers; trying to take a coin out of a purse to put into a pay-phone without putting down the receiver; trying to get a key off a stiff keyring.
   When ready, they join with another group; in turn, each mimes its difficulties to the other. The observing group tries to work out *as precisely as possible* what the difficulty is. Questions and comment should be encouraged.
   The activity may then be repeated, using large instead of small objects.

Remarks

Level: elementary upwards.
   With exercises such as this – in which the focus is on *the observa-*

tion of action – it is essential that the students have a clear idea of what they are trying to do. It is not enough, for instance, to mime merely the action of threading a needle without knowing *why* one is doing so. At the preparatory stage, therefore, the students should be encouraged to put their ideas in writing – and possibly even to exchange slips of paper. If this is done, the quality of the mime will improve, and hence the quality of the language as well, for the language depends directly on the action observed.

See also 2.9 Taste, touch, smell, 3.1 Exchanging objects, 3.17 What am I doing?, 3.24 Tableaux, section 8 A day's work.

2.17 Kim's game

What to do

For this exercise, a collection of disparate objects is needed – about fifteen in all. These might be, for instance, a light-bulb, a screwdriver, a used railway ticket, a foreign coin, a bar of soap, etc. With classes larger than fifteen, two collections of objects will be needed.

The objects are placed on a long table (on two tables for larger classes), so that they can be seen by everyone. The students examine the objects for three minutes. The table is then covered, and everyone goes off to jot down as many objects as he or she can recall. About five minutes are allowed for this. Before the objects are uncovered, each student calls out one object from his or her list, so that a second – oral – list is now established. Then the cover is taken off.

The exercise is now repeated, but this time the students are told to look carefully at the *size, shape, colour,* and disposition of the objects. The objects are again covered. This time, however, the students do not work alone but reconstitute their lists with a partner. (Their old lists should not be referred to.) At least ten minutes should be allowed for this, and *both* partners write out their joint list, noting if they wish any points of disagreement. Details should be as accurate as possible: size, for instance, can be better expressed in relative than in general terms, e.g. 'the matchbox is a half as long as the bar of soap', rather than merely 'the matchbox is small'.

Once a pair has exhausted its joint memory resources, the partners split up and look for someone else with whom to compare lists. They should try to see at least four other people.

The objects are now, at last, uncovered, and the lists compared with the collection on the table.

Remarks

Level: elementary upwards.

A collection of everyday objects is of no especial interest in itself. However, as we have seen in earlier exercises, as soon as the familiar is removed from sight it becomes intriguing. With Kim's game, the interest generated can usually be sustained for a long time, which means that the activity can be taken at a fairly leisurely pace.

Paradoxically, the language requirements for this absorbing exercise are relatively modest. At the first stage, the students need only be able to identify the objects. And even if some of the nouns are unfamiliar (e.g. *nail-clippers*), they will soon become familiar through frequent repetition. In order to discuss the details, the students still need no more than certain common adjectives, comparatives and contrastive phrases. If they need a word which they do not know, e.g. *chipped*, they should be encouraged to find their own way of expressing it, for the chances are that they will in fact hear the word they need when comparing lists with other students.

For those working with more advanced groups, an element of the unexpected can be introduced by altering (surreptitiously) some of the objects while the students are working in pairs compiling their descriptive lists. So, for instance, a blue ball-point can be exchanged for the red one; the position of the theatre ticket can be altered; the matchbox can be removed altogether; the 500-lire note can be changed for a 1000-lire note, and so on.

See also 2.3 Observation of the room, 2.14 If I remember rightly...

2.18   Lost memory

What to do

This exercise can be done only in pairs. The organizer should therefore take part if necessary. In each pair, one person has been found walking the streets late at night. He or she is completely lost and does not seem to remember anything. This person must be taken *home* by the other. (It is, therefore, best for students not to work with close friends.) The person who is suffering from loss of memory is also very weak, and must be led carefully through the streets. Any obstacles should be pointed out: 'Watch out for the step...Give me your hand, it's slippery here', etc. Once they reach home, the stranger should be shown round, told where everything is (television, armchair, etc.). He or she should be given a physical sense of the apartment.

Once the guest is comfortable, the host should try to find out by questioning who he or she is and where he or she comes from. The host may need to help the guest's memory by showing him or her things, e.g. photos, ornaments etc. Slowly, together, they build up this person's past.

Remarks

Level: intermediate upwards.

Two distinct stages are involved in this exercise. It is essential, therefore, to allow plenty of time for the relationship to develop. (If necessary, hold back the instructions for the second stage until it is clear that each guest has a clear mental picture of the kind of apartment he or she is in. He or she should know, for instance, where the windows are, which rooms the doors lead to, where the light switch is, etc.). In the second stage, the guest is of course inventing his or her past. The host will need to ask many questions, but not all of these can be answered. In turn, the guest may wish to ask questions of the host. But the pattern of the conversation will vary from pair to pair.

See also 1.56 and 1.57 Childhood memories (1 and 2), 2.3 Observation of the room, 2.8 Familiar scenes, 2.13 From my album, 7.9 Amnesty.

3 Interpretation

3.1 Exchanging objects

What to do

The students sit either in long rows or in pairs facing each other. Each thinks of an object, and attempts to visualize its shape, size, weight, etc. After two or three minutes, one partner in each pair shows the other, using simple *mime only*, what object he or she has in mind. Then his or her partner does the same. No words are exchanged at this stage.

Each now hands over his or her own object to the other person, i.e. each receives the other's object. Both now discuss what they think they have received.

The pairs then break up, and new groups of three are formed. Each group works out a short sketch involving each of the three objects earlier received.

Remarks

Level: elementary upwards.

Here, a real world is being created out of thin air. Done with care, this can be a most rewarding exercise, as it shows in the simplest possible way how unimportant physical 'props' are in drama activities. It is therefore an excellent preparatory exercise for getting students used to the idea of *creating their own material*.

Notice also the interesting progression here from simple identification to the language of discussion and interpretation.

See also 2.16 Difficulty with large or small objects, 3.17 What am I doing?

3.2   Things aren't what they seem to be

What to do

The class is divided into pairs. Each pair has a chair. Their task is to decide together on five or six things this chair might be or represent, other than 'something to sit on', for instance: a wheelbarrow, a machine-gun, a TV-aerial, etc. They then work out very brief mime sketches to illustrate these ideas. When ready, the pairs circulate and perform to others.

A variant of this exercise is to give each pair a different object, e.g. a wastepaper basket, a cushion, an ashtray, etc., provided this is practically possible.

Remarks

Level: elementary upwards.

Apart from its usefulness for practising speculative language ('I think...', 'It might be...', 'It looks as if...' etc.), this activity is excellent preparation for the later, more complex, mime exercises. It demonstrates – more convincingly than words alone – how easily the everyday world can be transformed, and how the familiar can be made to lose its familiarity. It also reminds us that the world is as we choose to see it!

See also 2.16 Difficulty with large or small objects, 4.1 The all-purpose sock, 4.5 Cork, stone and wood, 4.8 Fashion show, section 8 A day's work.

3.3   What time of day is it?

What to do

The class is divided into groups of two or three. Each group decides on a time of day and a character, e.g. 04.30, a Scout leader; 17.45, a mannequin. The character then performs an action appropriate to the time of day, e.g. blowing the bugle, posing for the press photographers. Each group performs its mimes to at least two other groups.

With experienced groups, this first stage can be omitted. In the second stage, the groups write down their suggestions on separate slips of paper, adding in a third element – place, e.g. 09.00, a restaurant waiter, Tahiti. Three separate piles are now made: person, time, place. Each group draws one slip at random from each pile. The task is now to work out a sketch involving all three elements.

Remarks

Level: elementary to intermediate upwards.

With inexperienced groups, it is probably wisest not to go beyond the first stage, as the language demands here are still very modest. With intermediate groups, both stages should be tried: the first in order to give a firm, 'realistic' basis for the more imaginative and less predictable developments in the second.

See also 3.28 Tension, 4.17 People, places, problems and things, 6.4 Faces and places.

3.4   **What am I wearing?**

What to do

Each person in the group is asked to write down three unusual or interesting professions on a slip of paper (e.g. deep-sea diver, clown, oyster-cultivator) – these should preferably be non-sedentary professions. The slips of paper are then placed in a pile, and each student draws three.

Working in groups of three, the students now mime to each other the *footwear* that might be worn by people with the professions they have chosen. The others in the group try to guess the profession. The same can then be done for *headwear*, this time without working from suggestion slips.

The groups now break and re-form, so that everyone is working with two new partners. This time, the groups of three work out a short sketch, in which each person mimes putting on or taking off a complete outfit (the three need not necessarily be linked, e.g. a judge preparing for a trial, an astronaut preparing to enter the gravity-free chamber, a striptease dancer dressing after the show). When ready, each group performs to others.

Remarks

Level: elementary upwards.

Again, familiar objects and actions are being used to accustom the students to recreating the real world through fantasy. In the third stage, it is important that each person in the group should try to help the others by offering advice and comment. In this way – even though their mimes are different – they will be working together as a group when performing to others.

See also 3.17 What am I doing?, 4.8 Fashion show.

3.5 Split headlines

What to do

Material needed: newspaper headlines (see examples below). The headlines are cut into two parts, e.g. CAN THIS PLAN and SAVE VENICE? Each person in the class is then given one half of a headline, and told to *memorize* the words. Everyone now circulates, saying his or her words aloud to everyone else. The purpose is to find as many partners as possible, i.e. anyone whose half-headline *could* fit either before or after your own. Once everyone has spoken to everyone else, the possible combinations are discussed by the class as a whole. It is only at this stage that any attempt is made to find the 'correct' solutions.

Remarks

Level: intermediate upwards.

This might be called an exercise in 'intuitive grammar', i.e. the ability to *predict language patterns* from minimal clues. It should therefore be made clear from the start that the aim is not to find the one 'correct' combination, but as many plausible combinations as possible. The skill practised here is one which is also needed in *listening* to a foreign language, i.e. picking up clues to meaning from the patterns used by the speaker.

The advantage of this activity is that the material can be selected beforehand, and therefore – particularly with less advanced classes – any cultural, lexical or grammatical difficulties can be eliminated.

It should also be remembered that time must be allowed for *discussion* of the various possible combinations.

See also 3.6 Split exchanges, 3.8 Jumbled stories, 4.12 Strange news, 5.7 Odd news.

EXAMPLES OF SPLIT HEADLINES

WHY PETROL	PRICES NEED NOT RISE
CAN THIS PLAN	SAVE VENICE?
WHO IS TO BLAME? AND	WHAT SHOULD BE DONE?
IS LONDON	CHOKING TO DEATH?
OUR SPY STORY	IS GAGGED
NASTY FOR YOU AND ME	NICE FOR INDUSTRY
BRITONS KNOW LITTLE ABOUT	SEA FOOD
STAY IN BED AND	CALL THE POLICE
MEET THE LEADING LADY	OF SOLIDARITY

Note: with stronger groups, punctuation marks – particularly question marks – may be left out. This broadens the range of possibilities. Students may be told that they can insert a question mark if they feel it is appropriate.

3.6 Split exchanges

What to do

Samples of the material needed are given below.

Each student is given one *half* of a dialogue exchange, e.g.
- Male ostriches are supposed to be very devoted fathers.
- So are foxes

or – I've just got back from Bulgaria.
- How very interesting.

The students are given half a minute to *memorize* what is written on the slip of paper. The whole class then circulates freely, each person saying aloud *only* the words given and listening carefully to what is said by the others to see if anyone has a sentence that *might* match theirs. It is essential, however, that everyone should speak to everyone else, and not simply search for one possible partner.

At least five minutes should be allowed for this. Then, those who think they have found partners move to one side of the room, those without partners to the other. Those who have found no partner call out their half of the exchange to the whole group. Invariably, two or three people will be found whose exchanges might 'fit'.

Remarks

Level: elementary upwards.

This might be considered as a warming-up exercise for other activities in this section. In addition to being a diverting ice-breaker, however, it is also an excellent on-the-spot test of understanding. Every time a student exchanges a sentence with another, he or she is doing all of the following: comparing several sets of structures and judging whether they could be logically (or grammatically) combined; imagining a possible context for these utterances; adjusting intonation to fit the possible meaning of his or her partner's sentence; gradually realizing that words do not necessarily have one meaning only – that the same words can mean different things in different combinations. The student is, then, calling upon his or her full understanding of the language, even though the choice of structures and vocabulary may be extremely restricted.

This exercise may also be extended by suggesting that the students expand the exchanges, working either with a suitable partner or in groups of four. As in 3.11 Dialogue interpretation, here too they should work out what might have been said immediately before and after the exchange.

See also 3.11 Dialogue interpretation (for full cross references), 3.5 Split headlines, 5.8 News poems.

EXAMPLES OF SPLIT EXCHANGES

There's a parrot in the fridge!
A parrot? Impossible!

Do you know what myxomatosis is?
Something to do with rabbits, I think.

I'm sorry, sir, but you can't go in there!
Do you realize who I am!

Would you like me to wrap it up for you?
Don't worry. I'll take it as it is.

I've got a splinter in my big toe.
Would you like me to take it out for you?

O that this too too solid flesh would melt...
Are you quoting again?

I've got five quid on 'Thunderbird' to win.
You're just throwing your money away!

Have you ever been convicted of a serious offence?
It depends what you mean...

Have you ever had malaria?
No, why do you ask?

Didn't I see you at the Casino last night?
No, you didn't!

I thought you said you were getting married.
Not till after Christmas.

Have you heard the one about Brezhnev, Carter, and the parrot?
I might have...I'm not sure.

3.7 Mixed sets

What to do

When introducing this exercise for the first time, it is advisable to prepare the material in advance. On all subsequent occasions, this can be done by the class.

Material needed: several sets of cards containing facts which are closely enough related to form a natural unit. For instance: 1914, Sarajevo, Archduke Ferdinand, Assassination; or: Bartók, Kodály, Liszt, Dohnyány. These may all be related to the same subject area, or chosen from quite different fields (mathematics, history, painting, etc.). Below is a list of ideas for mixed sets.

The cards are shuffled. Each person is given one card. He or she should remember what is written on it, and go round the class trying to find three other people with whom to form a set. (It is advisable to have in reserve a few sets of three or five, in case there are odd numbers.) Clearly, the groups cannot form until everyone has spoken to everyone else.

Usually four or five groups will detach themselves fairly rapidly. At this stage, it may be more effective to stop the exercise and ask those who have not found anyone to go with them to say what was on their cards. The others should all listen. This may result in some reshuffling of groups.

Remarks

Level: intermediate upwards.

This is an extremely useful exercise for students whose main interest happens to be a subject other than language (e.g. catering, engineering), as it enables material from their primary subject to be introduced. The information on the cards need not be restricted to single words, or even to words at all. Figures and symbols can also be used. As described above, the exercise is fairly simple. It can be made more interesting, however, by introducing *overlap* between the sets. This means that certain cards might fit into more than one set, e.g. *Shakespeare* might belong to sets 8 or 9 below, and *metamorphosis* to sets 10 or 11.

See also 5.13 As mixed as a metaphor, 6.5 Split cartoons, 6.9 Maps.

IDEAS FOR MIXED SETS

1 Many hands make light work.
   Too many cooks spoil the broth.
   Look before you leap.
   A stitch in time saves nine.

2 A bird in the hand is worth two in the bush.
 Birds of a feather flock together.
 One swallow doesn't make a summer.
 Don't count your chickens before they hatch.

3 Gold. Silver. Diamond. Anniversary
4 Ruby. Sapphire. Turquoise. Emerald
5 Limpopo. Amazon. Zambesi. Nile
6 Rhone. Danube. Rhine. Tiber (all rivers in Europe)
7 Thames. Anglia. BBC. Yorkshire (all television stations in England)
8 Caesar. Brutus. Antony. Rome
9 Shakespeare. Elizabeth I. Sir Francis Drake. Francis Bacon
10 Metamorphosis. Translation. Alteration. Transformation
11 Psychosis. Osmosis. Plasmolysis. Democracy (all words of Greek origin)
12 Plough. Through. Rough. Thorough
13 Borough. Burrow. Borrow. Barrow
14 Outlet. Outcast. Outbreak. Outrage
15 Outcome. Issue. Consequence. Result

3.8 Jumbled stories

What to do

The class should be divided into several large groups, seven to ten per group. Each group will be given a story in fragments. (Examples are given below of stories that might be used.) Each member of the group is given a slip of paper on which part of the story or incident appears. As this is an *oral* exercise, the fragments of the story should be memorized. The group's task is to reconstruct the story. In order to make this task more difficult, however, each group is given *two* fragments of the story another group is working on. All that the groups need be told is: 'each of you has the fragment of a story; read and memorize your fragment, then, by *talking* to the others, try to find out where it fits into the story. Remember that *two* of the fragments belong to the story of another group.'

About ten minutes are allowed for discussion. Each group is told that they can offer the fragments they do not want to another group. An exchange can be made only if both groups agree that they want the fragment offered. (Clearly, this works best if there are more than two groups.)

With groups of advanced students, it is possible to make the exercise more difficult by using longer stories and holding back several fragments of the story. The groups are then asked to *predict* what will be said in the phrases they need. If their predictions are reasonably accurate, they are given the missing fragment.

Finally, if time allows, each group can present its story as a mime. The observers try to build up the details by commenting as the mime goes on.

Remarks

Level: intermediate upwards.

Here, the language *content* is controlled, but the discussion is free. Much careful *listening* will have to be done, and there will be much repetition of phrases. This may be considered as a more complex version of 3.6 Split exchanges.

See also 3.22 Picture sets, 7.2 The time has come, 7.4 Starters.

EXAMPLES FOR JUMBLED STORIES

The worst tourist

The least successful tourist on record is Mr Nicholas Scotti of San Francisco. In 1977 he flew from America to his native Italy to visit relatives.

En route the plane made a one-hour fuel stop at Kennedy Airport. Thinking that he had arrived, Mr Scotti got out and spent two days in New York believing he was in Rome.

When his nephews were not there to meet him, Mr Scotti assumed that they had been delayed in the heavy Roman traffic mentioned in their letters. While tracking down their address, the great traveller could not help noticing that modernization had brushed aside most, if not all, of the ancient city's landmarks. He also noticed that many people spoke English with a distinct American accent. However, he just assumed that Americans got everywhere. Furthermore, he assumed it was for their benefit that so many street signs were written in English.

Mr Scotti spoke very little English himself and next asked a policeman (in Italian) the way to the bus depot. As chance would have it, the policeman came from Naples and replied fluently in the same tongue...

... Scotti's brilliance is seen in the fact that even when told he was in New York, he refused to believe it. To get him on a plane back to San Francisco, he was raced to the airport in a police-car with sirens screaming. 'See,' said Scotti to his interpreter, 'I know I'm in Italy. That's how they drive.'

The ugliest building ever constructed

In 1955 the British Ministry of Defence erected a reinforced concrete blockhouse in Scotland which was so ugly that planting a forest round it was later made a condition of sale. In 1975 the Ministry told Lord Cawdor, on whose land it was built, that the Army had no further use for it. He then had the problem of how to sell a single-storey grey concrete blockhouse, 175 feet long by 85 feet wide, with no windows, a box design, one camouflaged door and a flat roof.

In a newspaper advertisement he said, 'For sale: Reinforced concrete eyesore. Would suit nervous spy or mushroom farmer with dangerous wife for whom outhouse with five foot walls ideal. Offers and suggestions, however inane, invited for monument to corrupted endeavour. Forest planting a condition of sale.'

(Both extracts from *The Book of Heroic Failures* compiled by Stephen Pile)

3.9 Telephone conversations

What to do

A recording of one side of a telephone conversation should be made. (An example is given below. Further examples can be heard on the cassette accompanying *Variations on a theme*.)

The recording is played twice to the class as a whole. The first time the students simply listen; the second time they jot down what they think is being said at the other end of the line.

They then form pairs and work out the full conversation together (adding, if they wish, to the beginning and end). This is most effectively done sitting back-to-back.

When they are ready, they work with another pair, listening to and commenting on each other's conversation.

Here is a typical fragment:

A: ... Oh, no, just small ones... Well, we didn't have time really, and it *was* the rainy season... No, no trouble at all... Mmmm.... Listen, I was wondering if your mother would mind if we left them in the flat this evening... No, her flat!... Oh... No, nothing like last time, I promise... Well, we need the bath-tub really, because the kitchen sink's too small... Would you?... Thanks so much...

Remarks

Level: intermediate upwards.

Telephone conversations offer an excellent starting-point for improvisation. They also, incidentally, help students to project their voices and enunciate clearly, skills often passed by in classroom exercises.

In real life, we can never fully predict the course of a telephone conversation, although we are certainly able to influence its direction; here, too, we are free to say what we like, but constrained by whatever is said in reply. The ability to react, and react quickly, is essential if one is to become fluent in the foreign language.

See also 3.6 Split exchanges, 3.11 Dialogue interpretation, Maley and Duff: *Variations on a theme* (see Bibliography).

3.10 One-word dialogues

What to do

Material needed: a number of dialogues made up of one-word utterances, e.g.

A: Good.	A: Food.	A: Liver.	A: Speak up.
B: Good?	B: Food.	B: Kidney.	B: Hush!
A: Good.	A: Drink.	A: Liver!	A: Hush?
B: Well...	B: Drink.	B: Kidney!	B: Yes...
	A: Cigarette?		
	B: No.		

These are given out to students working in pairs – one dialogue for each pair. (At least two pairs must have the same dialogue, but it does not matter if several pairs have the same dialogue.)

Their first task is to decide *who* is talking, *where* they are, *what* they are talking about.

The pairs then join to form groups of four (with pairs which have the same dialogue as themselves), in which they compare their interpretations. Once they have agreed on one interpretation, they expand the dialogue by lengthening the utterances and by continuing the exchanges if possible.

Groups then perform their dialogues for other groups.

Remarks

Level: elementary upwards.

Apart from the opportunity this gives for interaction, the activity also has value in highlighting the polyvalence of words and the importance of *total context* in interpreting what is said.

Care should be taken to encourage pairs (and groups) to seek out a number of possible interpretations, and not to go for the easiest option.

See also 7.4 Starters, Maley and Duff: *Variations on a theme* (see Bibliography).

3.11 Dialogue interpretation

What to do

The students are given a short sentence, such as 'Where are you going?', and told to think of a person who might say this and a possible reason for saying it. They then walk round the room, trying out their sentence on others and listening to and commenting on the other versions they hear.

While they are busy working on this, a brief exchange – preferably one which might be variously interpreted – is written up on the board or on a display panel, e.g.

A: A man came to see you.
B: Oh? When?
A: While you were out.
B: What did he want?
A: He didn't say.

Working in pairs, the students should now decide on a possible setting for this fragment – who it might have been spoken by, where, and why. Once these details have been settled, each pair should run over the dialogue, adding if necessary to the beginning or end, but *not changing* the central core. When ready, they try out their dialogue on other pairs. Each pair tries to guess as much as it can about the context of the dialogue it hears.

As a follow-up to this activity, the students can also 'flesh out' a short dialogue, i.e. decide what might have been said before and after, and create a short sequence of which the original dialogue is part. This time they may tamper with the wording of the original.

Suggestions for dialogue openings are given below. Further suggestions, and alternative ways of using dialogues, can be found in *Variations on a theme* by the present authors (see Bibliography).

Remarks

Level: intermediate upwards.

In the previous two exercises, the students are getting used to the idea that the meaning of a sentence depends only partly on the words. As soon as they begin to work together, they will realize how much the full meaning depends on intonation, stress, strength of voice, bodily and facial movement, and on the personality of the partner.

Much dialogue material in text-books is fabricated so as to allow for only one interpretation – the 'right' one. In this activity, the only right interpretation is the one the students give themselves.

See also 1.31 Listening, 3.6 Split exchanges, 3.10 One-word dialogues, all of section 5 Word-play, 7.2 The time has come, 7.4 Starters.

SUGGESTIONS FOR DIALOGUE STARTERS

1 A: And that's when I told him.
   B: That was brave of you.

2   A: Well I must say I *am* surprised!
   B: Yes, I thought you would be.
   A: But what are they going to do about it?

3   A: As much as that? But was it worth it?
   B: Well, you know her as well as I do.
      Once she's made up her mind...

4   A: Well after that, what more could I say?
   B: Mm. I can see it must have been difficult for you.
   A: Difficult!

3.12   Interviews (2)

What to do

Material needed: specimens of interviews with famous people. These can be read at home as preparation for this exercise. The students should be asked to note the typical questions, to decide what order the questions most often follow, and to pick out examples of difficult questions.

Now, each member of the class is given a portrait (see examples below). Working in pairs, the students discuss each other's portraits. They should decide as much as they can about the personalities of the two figures. Then they draw up several interview-type questions they would like to ask those people. (In their discussion, they should also try to imagine the answers.) This takes about ten minutes.

Each person should now complete his or her list of questions. The pairs break up, and each person goes to a different partner. One is to be the interviewer, the other the person interviewed. The latter puts his or her portrait in a place where it can be seen by the interviewer, and answers the questions 'for' the person in the portrait. The interviewer may use his or her list of questions, but does not have to. He or she can invent questions as the interview proceeds. Each person should both interview and be interviewed.

Remarks

Level: advanced.

The initial preparation in pairs is important as it allows time for each person to reflect about his or her portrait. Without this, it would be extremely difficult to go 'cold' into the interview. The organizer may choose to give the instructions in *two* stages, so that the class does not in fact know how the questions that are being drawn up will be used later. The organizer may also suggest that the portraits be

kept face down, and shown only at the end of the interview. Like this, the person being interviewed is required to 'become' the figure in the portrait rather than merely lend his or her voice.

See also 1.49 Interviews (1), 3.19 Portraits (2), 3.20 Becoming a picture.

3.13 Palmistry, the zodiac and fortune-telling

What to do

a) In pairs, the students study the diagram and text set out below. They then take turns to look at each other's hands and interpret the lines they see.

b) In groups of four, they read the chart below, then discuss whether each person in the group corresponds with the description of his or her sign.

c) One person from each group is now sent to another group to ask which signs its members were born under, and returns to his or her own group with the information. The group then writes horoscopes for the day for the people concerned. Groups then give back the horoscopes for discussion.

d) An alternative development is for students to work in groups of four or five. Each person has the zodiac chart. No one must reveal his or her sign. Everyone in turn then performs a mime to convey the information contained in his or her sign description.

Remarks

Level: intermediate upwards.

These are just some of the ways in which palmistry and the zodiac can be used to stimulate discussion and lead to drama. Even if people do not 'believe' in the signs, they exert a continuing fascination.

See also 1.44 What's in a hand?, 1.66 Same/different, 4.6 Something in common (2), 5.11 The oracle.

Palmistry

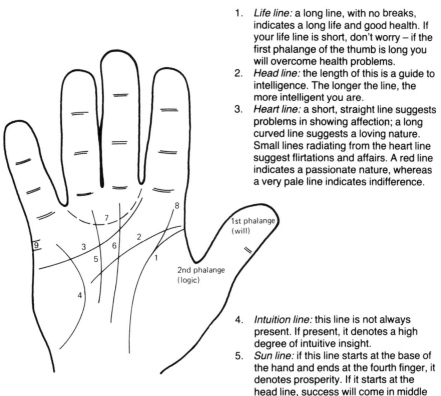

1. *Life line:* a long line, with no breaks, indicates a long life and good health. If your life line is short, don't worry – if the first phalange of the thumb is long you will overcome health problems.
2. *Head line:* the length of this is a guide to intelligence. The longer the line, the more intelligent you are.
3. *Heart line:* a short, straight line suggests problems in showing affection; a long curved line suggests a loving nature. Small lines radiating from the heart line suggest flirtations and affairs. A red line indicates a passionate nature, whereas a very pale line indicates indifference.
4. *Intuition line:* this line is not always present. If present, it denotes a high degree of intuitive insight.
5. *Sun line:* if this line starts at the base of the hand and ends at the fourth finger, it denotes prosperity. If it starts at the head line, success will come in middle age; starting at the heart line, happiness will come late in life.
6. *Fate line:* if the line starts at the wrist and continues up to the third finger, it indicates success as a reward for hard work.
7. *Girdle of Venus:* if present, it suggests sensitivity and enthusiasm.
8. *Ambition line:* the point at which this line diverges from the lifeline shows how early or late in life your ambitions will be realised.
9. *Marriage lines:* the closer to the heart line these are, the sooner you will marry.

Aquarius Jan. 20 – Feb. 18
Aquarians are intelligent and inventive. They tend to be able to detach themselves from their surroundings and other people. They have problems, however, with their blood circulation, throat and ankles. When choosing a career they should look in the areas of mechanics, teaching, politics and writing.

Pisces Feb. 19 – March 20
Those born under the sign of the fish are sensitive and understanding. They are also unpredictable in their behaviour. They suffer from nervous tension and have problems with their digestion. They are best suited to careers in music, writing, painting and pharmacy.

Aries March 21 – April 20
Those born under this sign are very active people. They are impulsive and they can be overpowering. Their health problems tend to be high blood pressure, migraine headaches and kidney disease. They often choose engineering, hairdressing or sales as a career.

Taurus April 21 – May 20
Taurans are reliable, practical people but they can be rather stubborn in their dealings with people. Their most common health problem is with the throat and blood circulation. They should look for careers in architecture, beauty and accounting.

Gemini May 21 – June 20
The twins are versatile and lively. They like to chat, but are restless and are always looking for new things. They are also nervous and suffer from rheumatism and lung complaints. They show most ability in careers in law, advertising or sales.

Cancer June 21 – July 21
Those born in Cancer are loyal to their friends and very sensitive. They can also be moody, however. Their physical weak points are to be found in the stomach, breast and kidneys. They should excel at shopkeeping, designing and clerical work.

Leo July 22 – Aug. 21
Leos have generous and confident personalities though they can be egotistical and sometimes arrogant. They can have problems with the throat, heart and spine. They should choose teaching, acting or management as a career.

Virgo Aug. 22 – Sept. 21
People born under Virgo are thorough and careful. They are reasonable but can be very critical. They suffer from problems of the stomach and with rheumatism. When choosing a career they should consider teaching, book-keeping and writing.

Libra Sept. 22 – Oct. 22
Libras are elegant and tactful in their manner but often hesitant in dealing with people. They tend to have kidney complaints and trouble with ulcers. They are suited to careers involving clerical work, fashion and personnel management.

Scorpio Oct. 23 – Nov. 21
Scorpios are intense in their relationships, determined to get their own way and very jealous. They have problems with blood circulation and the back. They could choose a military career, medicine or mechanics.

Sagittarius Nov. 22 – Dec. 20
Sagittarians are independent but very friendly. They can also be outspoken in their opinions. Their medical weaknesses can be in the intestines, lungs and liver. Their choice of careers could be in teaching, writing or show-business.

Capricorn Dec. 21 – Jan. 19
Those born under the sign of the goat are ambitious but reserved. They are thorough in their approach to their work. They suffer from rheumatism, stomach complaints and allergies. Their career prospects are strongest in business, show-business or social work.

3.14 Inkblots

What to do

Material needed: a series of inkblots (as below). There should be enough for one between every two students. In pairs, they work out an interpretation of the inkblot. Then the pairs join to make groups of four and share their interpretations. They should be encouraged to offer alternative suggestions to each other's interpretations.

The group is then asked to put the four inkblots down on the floor, or on the table, in such a way that they form a connected story. When this has been done, one person from each group goes to the next one and tries to work out what the story is. He or she may ask as many questions as are necessary. Once the story has been worked out, he or she stays on with the group, and together they develop a short (two-minute) dramatization of their story, which is then acted out for one other group.

Remarks

Level: intermediate upwards.

It helps if the inkblots are not all the same basic shape. A little experimentation will show how much variety can be obtained. It will at times be necessary to apply gentle pressure to prevent students from opting for the facile interpretation ('It's a butterfly', 'a bat', etc.). Often by turning the blot upside down one can cause the interpretation to undergo a radical change.

With this caveat, it is extraordinary how such a minimal stimulus will give rise to such varied interpretations.

See also Maley, Duff and Grellet: *The Mind's Eye* Teacher's Book, p. 39 (see Bibliography), 3.22 Picture sets, 6.2 Boxed-in.

3.15 Unknown gadgets

What to do

In groups of four, the students are given a picture of an unknown gadget (see illustrations below). In a class of twenty-four, for instance, it is useful if three groups work on the same picture, and the other three on another.

The group's task is first to work out what the use of the gadget is, then to write out together a piece of publicity for it, describing its function and praising it at the same time.

In a final stage, two groups with different pictures merge and work out a brief dramatized incident which involves both their gadgets.

Remarks

Level: advanced.

The activity works just as well if all groups have different pictures. A further development, if the work is flowing easily, is to ask groups to devise an improbable gadget of their own and then to present it to the others.

See also 4.15 Patent pending, 4.16 Making a machine.

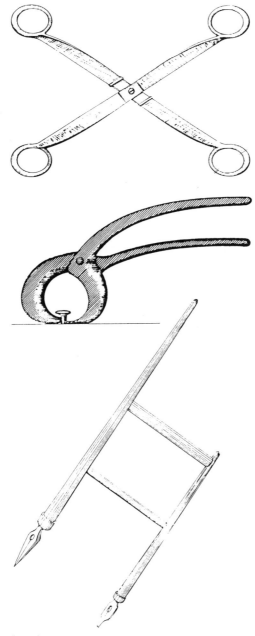

Unknown gadgets

3.16　High point

What to do

The students work in pairs. Each partner draws a picture of a particularly important moment in his or her life; one should concentrate on *a place*, the other on *a person*. When the drawings are finished, the pair should spend some time discussing them and finding out as much as possible about the incidents depicted.

Each pair then joins another pair with whom they exchange explanations of their respective pictures. The group thus formed then works out an improvised dramatization involving the two places and the two persons depicted.

Remarks

Level: elementary upwards.

Again, some students will object that they cannot draw. It will be necessary to persuade them that the main point is not to draw a perfect picture but to convey the essence of the incident.

See also 1.56 and 1.57 Childhood memories (1 and 2), 2.13 From my album, 3.19 Portraits (2), 4.7 It means a lot to me.

3.17　What am I doing?

What to do

As this exercise is conceived as an introduction to mime for students who may never have done any before, it is suggested that for the first few times the material be prepared in advance. Examples are given below.

Work is done in pairs. Everyone should have enough room to move about easily. Each member of the pair is given a slip of paper on which several actions are briefly described. He or she chooses one of the actions to mime. By using only bodily movement and sounds (but *not* words), partners take it in turn to show each other what they are doing (e.g. a tightrope walker crossing a waterfall and suddenly getting stomach-ache). The partner who is watching comments on the action and tries to work out all the details.

Remarks

Level: elementary upwards.

Although seemingly a strongly directed exercise, it is by no means restrictive. The members of each pair quickly forget the presence of the others, and become engrossed in their own work. It will be noticed that the standard of the mime rapidly improves as the exercise progresses. Depending on the receptivity of the group, it may or may not be necessary to remind them that all details should be shown, e.g. 'If *you are a deep-sea diver fighting with an octopus*, it should be an octopus and not just "a fish".'

The examples below have been loosely based on certain standard movements with variations, e.g. various ways of walking, sitting, looking, etc. Each set of movements also contains at least one 'complex' mime, involving either a second or third person, or a historical figure. These ideas will at first sight seem 'impossible'. This is why it is best not to discuss them at all before the exercise. It happens only rarely that someone cannot get across his or her message, and, although it need not be explicitly mentioned, nobody is to know if one of the actions has been left out.

See also 2.16 Difficulty with large or small objects, 3.18 The hotel receptionist, 3.24 Tableaux, 4.16 Making a machine, section 8 A day's work.

EXAMPLES OF ACTIONS TO MIME

1 You are:
   - sitting on a frozen lake, fishing through a hole in the ice
   - sitting on the floor in the corridor of a crowded train
   - trying to keep awake during a boring lecture
   - lying in an uncomfortable couchette (top bunk)
   - a private detective, leaning against a lamp-post, watching...
   - sitting on the inside seat in a jumbo jet; you want to get up, but the person next to you has his or her head resting on your shoulder
   - Michelangelo, painting the roof of the Sistine Chapel

2 You are:
   - in a crowded bus, trying to read someone's newspaper
   - reading a complicated railway train-timetable, trying to work out if you will have to change trains or not
   - reading the news on TV
   - a medieval monk, writing (illustrating) a precious manuscript
   - a traffic police-man/woman, writing out a traffic fine
   - trying to read a seventeenth-century gravestone in a churchyard
   - Queen Elizabeth I/Winston Churchill, signing her/his name

3 You are:
   - trying to put the needle onto a certain place on a record
   - trying to eat spaghetti with your left hand (you are right-handed, but your arm is broken)
   - sitting in a crowded aeroplane, trying to tie your shoelaces
   - lying in bed, in the dark, trying to switch off an alarm-clock
   - high up in a cherry tree, picking the last cherries
   - a tightrope walker, half-way across the Niagara falls, when you get a terrible stomach-ache

4 You are:
   - a discus thrower at the Olympic Games, getting ready to throw
   - a lion-tamer in a circus, facing the lion
   - a Roman gladiator, looking up to Caesar to see if you should spare your opponent or kill him
   - an Egyptian belly-dancer in a night-club
   - watching a boxing match on television
   - the Mona Lisa, sitting for her portrait

5 You are:
   - trying to thread a needle in a railway train
   - blowing out the candles on your birthday cake (you are 9)
   - throwing darts in a pub
   - a film director, showing the hero and heroine how to kiss
   - trying to get back to your seat (in the middle of the row) after the play/film has already begun
   - Ben Hur, trying to win the chariot race

6 You are:
   - a gipsy violinist, playing in a Hungarian restaurant
   - a mountain-climber, trying to pull your friend up to the top
   - carrying a tray full of drinks at a crowded party
   - a parachutist, getting ready to jump
   - taking passport photos of yourself in an automatic machine
   - Romeo climbing onto Juliet's balcony/Cinderella trying on the glass slipper

7 You are:
   - blowing into a bag for a police breath-test on the main road
   - a ballet instructor showing a pupil how to do the 'entrechat'
   - at an airport, passing through the 'personal search' checkpoint
   - an artist, showing his or her model what pose to take
   - eating with (Chinese) chopsticks for the first time
   - trying to unscrew a tight cap on a bottle

8 You are:
  – a woodcutter, chopping down a large tree
  – a champion golfer, making a long shot
  – trying to carry a mattress upstairs by yourself
  – lying in bed in the dark, trying to catch a mosquito
  – dancing the tango with a partner who does not know the steps

3.18   The hotel receptionist

What to do

The kind of material needed for this exercise is shown below ('Example sentences'). Slips of paper, each containing no more than two sentences, should be prepared in advance.

Ideally, this activity should be done with the whole class forming one large group. With classes of more than seventeen, however, the students will have to be divided into two groups.

The group sits in a large horse-shoe formation. This horse-shoe represents the hotel reception desk (i.e. everyone, apart from the one performer, is the *receptionist*). A slip of paper is handed to one person in the group. This person should read the slip, memorize the request, and move to the open end of the horse-shoe to demonstrate in mime to the receptionist what his or her problem/desire/complaint is. The receptionist (i.e. the whole group) will try – by questioning – to discover what the voiceless guest wants to communicate. Under no circumstances may the guest use words – he or she is assumed to have temporarily lost the power of speech.

The guest continues miming until the *exact* contents of the message have been conveyed. So, for instance, if the slip of paper reads: 'I want to book a long-distance telephone call to Venice at 06.00 on Sunday. My room number is 101' – all the facts must be reproduced (Venice, not just any town, Sunday, not just any day).

Once the guest's message has been understood, he or she rejoins the reception group and someone else takes a turn. It is important that everyone be given a chance to act the guest, as it very often happens that the students who are initially most reluctant to perform in fact make very entertaining 'guests'.

Remarks

Level: elementary upwards.

This is an activity which must not be rushed. The first time it is tried, there will inevitably be some nervousness and stiffness, until the students come to realize that they are not performing to a potentially hostile audience, but simply working together as one group. It is important, therefore, that the receptionists should *all* participate. For this to happen, the guest will need not only to mime, but also to listen carefully to the suggestions thrown out, and to react to them with gestures indicating: 'Not quite...', 'You're warm...', 'No!', 'Yes, but what else...' etc. Left to itself, almost any group will develop its own gestures, which, as they become more stylized and more familiar, will help the activity to move more swiftly and economically.

Once the students have come to see the potential of the activity, the organizer might occasionally intervene to demand greater rigour, particularly at the end of each guest's performance, e.g. by insisting that the receptionists repeat the entire message before it is finally read out by the guest.

No matter what the message on the slip of paper may be, the questioning will almost invariably follow the same pattern: 1 establishing the key details ('You want to send a letter? You need stamps?'); 2 filling in the missing parts ('You want to send a registered letter?' 'To a country in the northern hemisphere?'); 3 tightening the screws ('You want *me* to post a registered letter to Finland for you?'). This means that it is possible to predict with considerable accuracy the language needed for this exercise; it is also possible to control the vocabulary by ensuring that the slips of paper contain only known (or only few unknown) words.

Below is a shortened outline of the typical pattern followed in this activity. Note the way in which the information gathered by the receptionists is built up, brick-by-brick, until the whole message is complete.

A variant of this activity, shown on British television, is to mime the titles of books, films, records or songs. This can be done in small groups of three or four.

See also 2.16 Difficulty with large or small objects, 3.2 Things aren't what they seem to be, 3.17 What am I doing?, 4.17 People, places, problems and things, 4.23 Masks.

OUTLINE OF TYPICAL PATTERN

Sentence on the slip of paper given to the guest:

I HAVE TO LEAVE EARLY IN THE MORNING. COULD YOU POST A REGISTERED LETTER TO FINLAND FOR ME?

Dialogue between the guest and the receptionist(s)

R1: You're leaving?
G: (nods)
R2: Tonight?

R3:   In the morning?
G: (nods)
R4:   You want stamps?
G: (gesture – 'Not quite')
R5:   You want to post a letter?
G: (gesture – 'Yes, but...')
R3:   You're going to the North Pole?
G: (gesture – 'Not *me!*')
R5:   You want to send a letter to the North Pole?
G: (gesture – 'Not so far north...')
R7:   Russia?
R8:   Iceland?
R9:   Denmark?
G: (gesture – 'Getting close')
R2:   Finland?
G: (nods firmly)
R7:   You want stamps for a letter to Finland?
R4:   You want to post a letter to Finland tomorrow morning?
G: (gesture – 'Almost')
R1:   You want *me* to post a letter to Finland tomorrow morning?
G: (gesture – 'Very close')
R9:   You're leaving tomorrow morning, and you want me to post a letter for you?
G: (gesture – 'Yes...just one more detail...')
R4:   A telegram?
R2:   An urgent letter?
R5:   A registered letter!

At this point, the guest indicates that this is correct, but the message must be repeated in its full and final form by the receptionists before the guest reads out his or her slip of paper.

EXAMPLE SENTENCES

1   I asked for a room with a view. I meant a view of the sea, not the car-park!
2   My wife/husband has been put in jail for taking a photograph of the statue in the main-square. I want to call my embassy.
3   My wife/husband is in bed with a bad hangover. Could you give me some Alka Seltzer.
4   How do you say 'Get lost!' in your language?
5   I want to book a long-distance phone call to Madrid for 22.00 hours this evening.
6   Don't think I'm mad, but every night a ghost comes into my room and sings 'Your tiny hand is frozen' (from *La Bohème*). I want to change rooms.
7   I found this note under my door this morning. Please could you translate it for me?
8   I don't like the pictures of the flying geese in our room. Please could you take them away!

9 Please could you send two vodkas up to room 303?

10 Have you got the TV-programme? I want to watch the wrestling.

11 A short fat man with a ginger-coloured beard has been following me in the street. If he asks where I am, say you have never seen me!

12 I want tickets for the rock-opera *Hamlet*. Can I get them here?

13 Can you tell me what time it is in New York, please?

14 Last night I was kept awake by mosquitoes. Please could you have my room sprayed!

15 Come quick! There's a flying-saucer landing in the car-park!

16 I want to go water-skiing tomorrow. Can I rent the skis from you?

17 The passport you gave me yesterday was the wrong one. I want mine back!

18 The hotel hairdresser gave me a shampoo. It's turned my hair blue! What are you going to do about it?

19 I lost my wallet at the aquarium this afternoon. Please could you phone and ask if they've found it?

3.19 Portraits (2)

What to do

Material needed: a collection of portrait photographs such as those used in 3.12 Interviews (2) (see p. 116 above). These pictures should show a person – preferably only *one* person – in close detail, and contain only a minimum of background. It is advisable to avoid portraits of well-known public figures.

Working in groups of three, the students study their portrait for four or five minutes, and then decide:
– how old the person might be
– what his or her profession might be
– whether he or she is married
– what he or she likes doing
– what he or she is doing at this moment
– what kind of person he or she is
One person in each group takes notes.

When one or two possible interpretations have been agreed upon, the group exchanges its picture with another group. After five minutes, the two groups meet to discuss their different impressions. The exchange is then repeated with other groups.

Remarks

Level: elementary upwards.

Many of the drama activities involve the study of character. This exercise serves as a useful introduction.

Most people, consciously or unconsciously, form opinions of others as soon as they see them. Here, we want to draw on this natural inclination in order to encourage the students to argue out opinions that would otherwise remain unformulated. Hence the importance of repeating the exchange of pictures with several groups.

See also 3.12 Interviews (2), 3.20 Becoming a picture, 3.21 Bringing a picture to life, 3.22 Picture sets.

3.20 Becoming a picture

What to do

This activity may be done individually, in pairs or in small groups (of about four). Photographs of the kind used in 3.12 Interviews (2) and 3.19 Portraits (2) would be suitable here, i.e. pictures of interesting-looking but *not* well-known people (see p. 116 above). Each student selects the portrait of someone he or she would like to become (the students might also be asked to bring their own pictures).

They now work for about twenty minutes on 'fleshing out' their pictures, i.e. building up as full a picture as possible of the person they are to become. The following questions should serve as a guideline:

The world of the picture
What is outside the frame of the picture?
What is beyond the horizon?
What lies nearby?
What is the scene shown?
What kind of a place is it? How does it look, smell, sound?
What do people do here?
What is this person doing here?
Who is nearby?

The person
Name, age, where born – city, country, family, where now?
Job/profession/trade/occupation/career?
When have you been the most happy?
What has made you most proud?

What do you look like: elegant, shabby, flamboyant, conservative, confident, anxious, ugly, defiant, withdrawn, plain?
What do you love, hate, admire, fear?
When did you leave home? Why? How?
When did you return?
Where do you live?
What brought you to this place?
Where are you going?
Who will be there?
How do you walk, sit, stand, speak, meet others?...

Each person, pair or group, then 'introduces' himself or herself either to other pairs or groups or to the whole class. This must be done in the first person ('My name is... I live... I was born in...' etc.) and without consulting any notes. The listener may take notes and ask supplementary questions afterwards ('What does your brother do?' 'Did you enjoy school?' 'What are you most afraid of?').

Remarks

Level: intermediate upwards.

This is a more highly developed version of the activities involving pictures in 3.19 Portraits (2) and 3.22 Picture sets.

One of the main problems is that some of the students will be reticent about 'putting themselves into someone else's skin'. For this reason, it may be worthwhile trying the exercise for the first time as a variant of 3.12 Interviews (2), in which the students all have to gather information about each other. In this exercise the information would, of course, relate to the person in the picture. The activity could then be extended by asking the students to form groups of four people with at least two things in common (in order to do this effectively, they would need to find out more and more information). Once formed, the groups would then work out a plausible story explaining how the four of them came to be acquainted – each student tells his or her own part of the story.

See also 3.12 Interviews (2), 3.19 Portraits (2), 3.21 Bringing a picture to life.

3.21 Bringing a picture to life

What to do

The exercise is done in pairs: each pair is given a picture, preferably one in which two people are present (see p. 97 above). The background of the picture should not be too complex. Together, they should try to recreate as accurately as possible the content of the picture. When ready, they 'perform' their picture to another pair. The spectators interpret what they see. Only after this are they shown the picture itself.

In the second part of the exercise students work in the same pairs, this time with a different picture. The picture should now be transformed to become an advertisement. Each pair has the right to add or take away any details. They should also write out a slogan to accompany the picture. When ready, they bring their picture to life for another pair, whose task is to guess what is being advertised. To conclude, each picture is presented to the class as a whole; this time, the original picture is also shown, and the slogan is given.

Remarks

Level: intermediate upwards.

Remember that people can 'become' objects in drama activities. This means that the pictures need not necessarily contain two people, although in the first part of the exercise it is advisable that they do. Cartoons and abstract or surrealist pictures can also be used.

This exercise gives rise to a considerable amount of discussion, both in the preparation of the picture and in the questioning during the stage of bringing to life.

See also 1.38 Becoming a musical instrument, 2.14 If I remember rightly..., 3.20 Becoming a picture, 3.24 Tableaux, 4.9 Statues.

3.22 Picture sets

What to do

In 2.14 If I remember rightly..., the groups worked on pictures to be memorized for detail. The same pictures may be used here. (See p. 97 above; further ideas may be drawn from *The Mind's Eye*, see Bibliography.)

Working in groups of four (exactly as in exercise 2.14), the students discuss their pictures. They then spread them out on the floor or on a table, and try to arrange them in a sequence so as to tell a story. It will certainly help to stimulate the imagination if at least two pictures in a set of five have some common element, e.g. two people talking, an elephant, rain on rooftops. One picture should be 'the odd man out', e.g. a single coloured picture in a set of black-and-white ones. There is, however, no need for students to be reminded to look out for common elements; this they will do of their own accord while working on the pictures.

Ten minutes – not more – are given for the preparation of the story. Each group then spreads its pictures out following the sequence in which they appear in the story. Two members from each group now move on to another group, and two remain behind with the pictures. The task of the newcomers to each group is to try to work out the story illustrated by the pictures. Their questions and suggestions should be answered by the two who know the story, but the answers should not be too explicit. Their task is not to retell the story, but to encourage the newcomers to work it out. Once they have finished, the newcomers remain with the pictures, and the two original members of the group move on to another.

The exercise can be concluded with each group telling its story to the whole class, holding up the pictures as they proceed.

Remarks

Level: intermediate to advanced.

So much useful language is produced during this activity that it is difficult to give more than a partial prediction of what will occur. What is particularly striking is the way in which the various stories alter and are altered or 'improved upon'. First, while the group is still trying to establish a sequence for the pictures, most of the language will be propositional: 'Couldn't he be waiting for her...? If we put this one first, the story could begin in the Sahara... What about making the man in the suit a figure from one of her dreams?' etc.

Once the story has taken shape and the group has started refining the details, the language changes to narration in the present; this occurs almost inevitably as the students are now describing what is happening in the pictures in front of them. Later, when others try to work out the story, the propositional language reappears.

In the final stage, with each group retelling its story to the whole class, the tenses become mixed, with past tenses predominating, as in 'normal' narration. In addition, at various stages in the activity, there will also be the language of criticism, disagreement, objection, etc. As this is truly an exercise in collective imagination, it almost invariably results in a high level of concentration and participation all round.

See also 2.14 If I remember rightly..., 3.8 Jumbled stories, 3.21 Bringing a picture to life, 3.26 The envelope, 4.11 Group story, 4.5 Cork, stone and wood, 4.12 Strange news, 5.10 Random dictionary, 7.3 Colourful ideas.

3.23 Talk of the Devil

What to do

This should not be attempted when the group is excited, restless, or in too high spirits. It is an exercise that requires concentration, the willingness to listen and think.

The class is divided into groups of three (one group of two or four if numbers are uneven). Each member of the group takes it in turn to talk freely about any person he or she knows well. This may be someone he or she likes or dislikes, but it should not be a well-known public figure. Rather than give a description of his or her relationship to this person, he or she should try to present an objective impression. This does not mean, however, that criticism or praise of that person should not enter into the description. One of the two listeners will take notes; the other will only listen. If A talks, B takes notes, and C listens. C will ask A to clarify any points he or she has not correctly understood and will offer suggestions as to what he or she thinks A's relationship to the person really is (and what A may be concealing). B will listen. When C has finished asking questions, B will compare what was said with the notes he or she took, adding comments and conclusions. This may take seven to ten minutes. It will now be B's turn to talk about someone; and so on.

Remarks

Level: intermediate to advanced.

The reason for saying that this should not be attempted when the group is excited is that one does not want it to degenerate into facile scandalmongering. Since the person being discussed is not present – and need never be known by name – this can be taken as an objective exercise in deduction. The speaker, inevitably, knows more than he or she tells. The interest is in seeing how much can be *deduced* from his or her manner of relating. B and C are trying to see behind the words.

This is a useful warming-up activity for work on portraits and other pictures, particularly 3.12 Interviews (2).

See also 2.15 I say, you said, he said, 3.19 Portraits (2).

3.24 Tableaux

What to do

Before the exercise begins, a single word – the theme – is written up on the board or announced. This might be a word such as *waiting, searching* or *observing* (in preference to more explicit or 'loaded' words, such as *anxiety, distress* or *fascination*). The class is divided into groups of four; each group works out a 'tableau' in mime around the theme.

Ten minutes are given for discussion of the idea, and five for preparation. When ready, the groups present their tableau to other groups. Each group should have time to see the work of all groups in the class.

Remarks

Level: elementary upwards.

The groups should be reminded – *during* rather than before the exercise - that it is essential for each person to have a clearly defined role in the tableau. Thus, for instance, if four people are waiting to see the vet, we should know who they are, how old they are, how long they have been there, what animals they have come with, etc. This is important because, as in all mime exercises, the clearer the initial idea the better the mime. And the better the mime the more likely it is to lead to worthwhile discussion. Over-preparation, however, should be avoided. This is why it is also important in this exercise to stick closely to the time limits, as the students will in fact be improving their tableau each time it is performed.

See also 3.21 Bringing a picture to life, 3.27 Conflict, 3.28 Tension, 3.29 Intruders.

3.25 Detective work

What to do

In 2.17 Kim's game, several objects were placed on a table for an exercise in memorization. The same objects may be used here, and this exercise may be done either independently or as a direct follow-on to Kim's game.

Half of the objects on the table are removed, and the remaining objects scattered freely over (and even around) the table. Working in pairs, as detectives, the students examine the objects – without·

changing their position – and then go off together to try to work out a plausible story (thriller?) in which all the objects figure. An added edge can be given by introducing a photograph or portrait among the objects.

Once a pair has worked out its story, both partners note the details and then go off separately to find another partner. The new partners exchange stories, listening carefully for any missing details, flaws in reasoning, or doubtful conclusions.

With large classes, two tables of objects will be needed.

Remarks

Level: intermediate upwards.

If the students are already familiar with the objects from Kim's game, they will have less difficulty in moving on to the more creative stage of devising a story. They will also enjoy discovering how, by this simple twist, fresh interest is given to the now familiar objects. What is important here is that they are now entirely in command of what they produce – it is *their* work, and this means they will take a personal interest in explaining and defending their stories.

See also 2.17 Kim's game, 3.23 Talk of the Devil, 4.6 Something in common (2), 5.7 Odd news, 5.10 Random dictionary, 7.10 Spring fever.

3.26 The envelope

What to do

Small groups of three or four are formed. Each group is given a large envelope. The members of each group now collect a number of small objects (e.g. coins, tickets, books of matches, nail-files, etc.) from their own pockets and bags. The group then selects ten to fifteen of these objects and imagines that they all belong to the same person. Together, they build up a story around this person. Explanations must be found for the connection each object has with this imaginary character. In order to provide a focus for the story, one may suggest that the objects are all 'evidence' that has been collected by the police.

When the groups have worked out the background of their characters, the objects are placed in the envelope and passed on to another group. Two of the members move on with the envelope and two remain behind. The newcomers – with the envelope – now reveal their objects and ask their new partners to try and work out the 'story' behind the evidence. They should answer direct questions, but not provide too much information of their own accord.

Remarks

Level: advanced.

As in many exercises, here we are working on building up a concrete situation from random elements. Ordinary and familiar objects are invested with fresh interest by being unexpectedly combined. The students' interest will be all the greater if they themselves provide the material.

See also 3.22 Picture sets, 3.25 Detective work, 4.5 Cork, stone and wood, 6.7 Alibi.

3.27 Conflict

What to do

a) The students work in pairs. One member of each pair is to be shop assistant, the other a difficult customer. The only instruction given is that the shop assistant should maintain self-control throughout, always responding politely and helpfully no matter how difficult the customer may be. Nevertheless, the tension between them should show.

   Five minutes are given for preparation. Details such as the age of the customer, the age of the assistant, and the kind of shop they are in (supermarket, small grocery store, airport boutique, etc.) should be clear in their minds before they begin. Together, they play out the situation, then repeat it again, this time exchanging roles.

b) Groups of four are now formed. Each group divides into two pairs, one pair taking the same situation as in (a). This time, however, the conflict is developed and allowed to come into the open; in other words, the shop assistant gradually reacts against the customer's attitude. The other pair observes the acting out of the situation, and offers comment and criticism when it is finished. The pairs then exchange places.

c) The students again work in groups of four, following the procedure in (b) above (one pair acting for the others to observe). This time, however, the groups should discuss other possible situations of conflict involving two people before deciding on one which suits them. Here are some possible conflict situations:
   – teenage girl wants to go abroad on holiday alone; mother is against the idea
   – he wants to leave the party; she wants to stay

- wife wants her ageing mother to come and live with her; husband is against it
- boss wants assistant to work over a weekend; assistant has promised to go to the country with his family
- young couple in a small flat; she wants to keep a dog, he wants a cat – or nothing!

Whatever the situation, the conflict level should be allowed to grow gradually from 'normal' to 'heated'.

d) The students form groups of six, each group being subdivided into two groups of three. The two sub-groups then decide on a subject of conflict between *two* people, and this is acted out. The third member of the group now intervenes to put an end to the conflict by pacifying the other two. As before, the other group of three first of all offers comment and criticism, then acts out its own situation.

Remarks

Level: intermediate upwards.

These interrelated exercises should have a pattern of development, and not be merely shouting matches. It is important, therefore, to insist on the need for a controlled growth of conflict.

Ideas for the conflicts – especially for (c) above – may be more readily forthcoming if a preliminary discussion is held with the whole class about the reasons for conflict between people.

See also 3.21 Bringing a picture to life, 3.28 Tension, 3.29 Intruders, 7.2 The time has come.

3.28   Tension

What to do

a) The class is divided into groups of three. Each group decides on a situation which involves *tension*. They then work out a silent scene to show the nature of the tension, for example:
- the wives of miners trapped underground waiting for news
- bank robbers holding up a cashier
- lovers having a quarrel
- a secretary sulking because her boss won't let her go early
- a man smoking in a non-smoking compartment
- someone behind you in the cinema rustling sweet papers
- waiting outside a phone-box for someone to finish a long conversation

— a bomb-disposal expert defusing a bomb

When ready, each group goes to another group and presents its scene. The other group has to interpret and comment on it. They then change places.

The groups then take the scene enacted by the group they have watched, and *add words to it*. They then present this scene to a group they have not yet worked with.

b) The class is divided into groups of five or six. Each group has to decide on a situation in which they are *threatened* by something but powerless to do anything, for example:
    — trapped miners hear the sound of water rising
    — passengers in a hijacked aircraft
    — passengers in an underground train which has stopped for an unusually long time in a tunnel
    — people trapped in a lift: someone smells gas
    — punters who have bet heavily on the favourite, waiting for the racing results on the radio

This should be prepared as a silent scene, which each group then shows to another group for interpretation and comment. As in (a) above, each group takes over another group's scene and *adds words*. This new scene is then shown to a different group. Discussion and comment follow.

c) The class is divided into groups of five or six. Each group is asked to work out a situation in which an *outsider* is involved, someone who for some reason does not belong. This time, words are used. Such situations might be, for instance:
    — someone who has not been invited to a party arrives when it is in full swing
    — one workman in a factory refuses to join in a strike
    — a vegetarian teetotaller attending a large banquet
    — a talkative neighbour drops in when everyone is tired
    — a group watching a film on TV; a latecomer keeps trying to find out what has happened

As before, each group performs for another group. Criticism and comment follow.

Remarks

Level: intermediate upwards.

These three interrelated exercises offer opportunities for the use of three different types of language: discussion/organization; performance/execution of ideas; criticism/interpretation, and again discussion.

The 'outside' activity can be extended to include other types of tension, e.g. by introducing the unexpected into a 'normal' situation: a family having breakfast – a poisonous snake suddenly appears.

The situations suggested here are only guidelines. It is preferable that the students devise their own ideas.

See also 3.24 Tableaux, 3.27 Conflict, 4.13 Starting from scratch.

3.29 Intruders

What to do

The class is divided into groups of five or six. Each group is given a slip of paper on which a situation is described in which a settled state of affairs is disturbed by the intervention of an intruder. The members of the group allot roles and work out in detail how they will play the scene. When they are ready they approach another group and play it out for them. This is followed by comment and criticism, after which the second group plays its own scene. Here are some ideas:

– A man arrives to repair a TV set. He completes the job, and while doing so, settles down to live in the flat.
– A waiter in a restaurant becomes so engrossed in recommending various dishes to his customers that he sits down with them. One of the customers ends up serving the meal.
– A solitary camper stops to ask a farmer for permission to put up his tent in the farmer's field. By morning a forest of tents has sprung up, and 'services' such as water, toilets, electricity, rubbish removal and catering are being demanded of the farmer.

Once the students have had some experience of this activity, the groups can be asked to work out their own intruder situations.

Remarks

Level: intermediate to advanced.

This is an activity which allows for a considerable variety of language at a wide range of levels. Very able students will tend to speak a lot and to stretch their knowledge. Less able students will not be discouraged because they too will be using their more limited language resources in a meaningful way.

See also 3.27 Conflict, 3.28 Tension, 4.18 Act Three.

3.30 Dream themes

What to do

The group needs to relax for this exercise: the relaxation could be done, for instance, lying on the floor in a circle, feet outwards heads inwards. (See 4.19 Waking dream.) For about two minutes, each person should try to recollect in as much detail as possible a recent dream. (It may help to play music, preferably *not* 'mood' music, during these two minutes.) All members of the group now circulate and exchange dreams: the purpose is to find someone whose dream contains some elements similar to those in one's own dream. Everyone in the group should try to talk to everyone else. This may take up to fifteen minutes, even more.

If time is left, one can suggest that smaller groups form, made up of those who have found similar elements in their dreams (these groups may range from two to five in size). Each group now makes a corporate dream sequence, which is then mimed to the others.

Remarks

Level: elementary upwards.

The imagination works seemingly without effort in dreams. This is why the dream can provide an extremely powerful stimulus for improvisation. If this exercise is to succeed, one needs to rethink the old cliché that 'other people's dreams are not interesting'.

See also 1.29 Relax, 1.30 Directed relaxation, 1.53 Group dream, 1.54 Directed group fantasies, 1.56 and 1.57 Childhood memories (1 and 2), 4.6 Something in common (2).

4 Creation and Invention

4.1 The all-purpose sock

What to do

Each student is asked to concentrate on a familiar object, e.g. a sock. The task is to draw up a list of six to ten ways in which a sock *might* be used other than for its normal purpose, for example:

a coffee-filter	a bandage
a trumpet-mute	a mask
a gag	a lamp-shade
a net	a purse

The group then forms pairs. Each pair exchanges ideas; about five minutes are allowed for discussion. At the next stage, two pairs join together to compare lists. A further five to ten minutes are allowed for this. Then each group is asked to describe to the others three (not more) of its best ideas.

The groups of four remain as they are. Each group is now asked to think of a similar everyday object (a hairpin, a comb, a fork, etc.). As before, a list of possible new uses for this object is drawn up. The group selects four of its best ideas and presents these as a mime to other groups. The observer group must try to decide what the object is and in what new way it is being used.

Remarks

Level: elementary upwards.

Although one is working here from a very simple idea, there is still great scope for the imagination. Some students will, of course, have more ideas than others: this is why the exchange of ideas in pairs is introduced. In the discussion, much useful language emerges when suggestions are compared, criticized, and rejected or accepted. The final stage – the mime presentation – is a complementary stage to 3.2 Things aren't what they seem to be.

See also 3.17 What am I doing?, 4.4 Potato figures, 5.10 Random dictionary, section 8 A day's work.

4.2 Emblems

What to do

The students work in groups of four. Each group is given a slip of paper with a single word, e.g. *candle, feather, cup, hook*. The same word should be given to two different groups. This means that if there are six groups, only three words will be used. The words chosen should not have any obvious symbolic connotations (e.g. words such as *star, hammer, sword,* and *sickle* should be avoided).

Each group is asked to turn its word into an emblem. This may be the symbol of a nation, a society, an association or a movement. They should decide on the history of their emblem (i.e. what events led to its being chosen), its meaning (i.e. what it represents), and its function (i.e. when and where it is used). They may of course add details to the final sketch, which should also include a written motto. The groups then pair off with those who have been working on the same word. Each presents its emblem to the other in as much detail as possible.

Remarks

Level: intermediate upwards.

In life, we are surrounded by symbols, designs, mottoes, emblems which – all too often – we ignore. This exercise not only offers an intriguing challenge to the students, but may also open up the way for interesting extensions in which symbols and designs are used in a different way.

See also 3.7 Mixed sets, 4.5 Cork, stone and wood, 4.25 Street demonstration, 5.11 The oracle, and the following four exercises in this section.

4.3 Signs of the future

What to do

The students work in pairs. Each pair is asked to imagine a city of the future. This city may, of course, be in space, underwater, underground, etc. They decide on the main features of this new civilization, and design signs and notices which a visitor to the city might see. Clearly, these signs will be meaningful only to the inhabitants. There should therefore be no recognizable words on them.

About twelve to fifteen minutes are allowed for preparation. Both partners make a copy of their sign (or signs). Now the pairs break up. Each finds a different partner. By guessing and questioning, they try to discover the meaning of each other's signs.

Remarks

Level: elementary upwards.

Like 4.15 Patent pending, this is an exercise in which drawing is used to divert the attention from language. The reason for doing this is that the students are learning to work together on something entirely of their own creation. In doing so, they are also discovering more about the way in which ideas come into being, i.e. ideas are seldom ready-made; they usually need polishing, changing. In some of the more complex exercises, e.g. 4.16 Making a machine, when they are working in larger groups, they will need the tolerance and understanding of others' ideas that exercises such as this help to bring out.

See also 3.14 Inkblots, 4.2 Emblems, 4.14 Amazimbi, 4.20 Music pictures, 6.2 Boxed-in.

4.4 Potato figures

What to do

Material needed: about 5 kg potatoes and a large quantity of matches. Students work in groups of four or five. Each group has a pile of ten to twelve potatoes. A handful of matches is given to each. Using the potatoes and the matchsticks, they should now construct a figure (or several figures) of their own choice. When the figures are finished, the groups break up and look at each other's work.

Remarks

Level: elementary upwards.

As in 3.2 Things aren't what they seem to be, the purpose of this exercise is to give fresh life to familiar objects. The ability to see ordinary things in a new light is one which needs to be developed if the more complex exercises (particularly those involving mime) are to succeed. This, then, is one of the exercises that may be considered as useful training. One point, however, should not be forgotten: in order to make a figure, the group must reach *agreement*. This will involve *rejecting* and *accepting* the suggestions of individuals.

See also 2.7 My potato, 4.20 Music pictures, 4.24 Visual consequences, 6.1 Castles in the air.

4.5   Cork, stone and wood

What to do

Material needed: enough corks, stones, and pieces of wood for every person in the class to have one of each. (Other materials, e.g. leaves, potatoes, bricks, might also be used.)

a)   The first stage is similar to 2.7 My potato. Large groups of ten to twelve are formed. A pile of corks, preferably almost identical, is placed in the middle. Each person takes one cork and turns away to examine it. After a minute, still with backs turned, students put the corks back into the middle. They then turn round and try to find their own corks. Comparison and discussion then follow.

b)   In the same groups: students are asked to close their eyes. A small stone is given to each person. Using only the sense of touch, they try to build up a picture of the stone, imagining what colour it is (all one colour, or striped?), how rough/shiny it is, and finally where it may have come from (a stream, a mountain path, etc.). They should try to identify with the stone and imagine some of the events in its 'lifetime'. Everyone is then asked to exchange his or her stone with the person on the right – still without opening their eyes. After a few minutes, the stones are returned. Now, with open eyes, they examine their stones and explain to others in the group what differences there were between the real and the imagined stone.

c)   The groups dissolve. Everyone now circulates freely, exchanging stories from the imagined lives of their stones. Each person will be looking in particular for someone who has a stone that is very similar or very different.

d)   Students form in groups of four. Each group already has four stones and four corks. They now receive four pieces of wood. Together (or in pairs) they should invent a short story or legend linking the stones, the corks and the pieces of wood. When the stories are ready, they should be exchanged.

e)   Students form different groups of four. Each group prepares an exhibition of its material, with short explanatory cards next to the objects (e.g. 'A Stone Age measure of weight', 'Fragment of a medieval torture instrument', 'A sacred object' etc.). The cards, however, should not explain too much. The groups now visit each other's exhibitions to hear in greater detail the history of the objects.

Remarks

Level: intermediate upwards.

Painters and sculptors are often inspired by the shape of natural objects, and even the most sluggish imaginations will have seen strange creatures in cloud formations, oil slicks, fallen tree trunks etc. In this exercise, the objects – particularly the stones and the pieces of wood – will often suggest their own stories. It is important, however, that during stage (b), when the stone is felt with the eyes closed, each person should try to 'become' that stone, to imagine how and where it used to lie, what things it could see around it, how it came to be moved, and where it would most like to be.

See also 1.22 Touch it, 2.5 Spot the change, 2.7 My potato, 3.1 Exchanging objects, 3.26 The envelope, 6.1 Castles in the air.

4.6 Something in common (2)

What to do

The first stage of this exercise is described in full in 1.51 Something in common (1). Here, we shall just briefly outline these instructions. Each person is asked to note down four things, e.g. a *superstition*, an irritating *machine*, a childhood *memory*, and a disagreeable *tic* or mannerism. The class then exchanges responses, with each person trying to find others with similar reactions.

In the second stage, groups of four or five are formed; in each group, there should if possible be two points in common, each of which is shared by two or more members of the group. (There may also be a group of those who have nothing in common with anyone else!) The groups are now asked to prepare a scene from a documentary film on, for instance, industrial safety measures, life insurance, or foreign trade. In the sequence they devise, one of each of the four elements must be introduced. This means that a group might come up with the following: a black cat, a pile-driver, buttered toast, and clicking the top of a ballpoint. These four elements must feature – even if transformed in some ways – in the sequence. The groups then present their sequences to the others, who will try to interpret what happens and identify the four elements.

Remarks

Level: advanced.

This exercise shows how little 'material' is needed to produce interesting work. The groups themselves supply the material and decide how they will work on it; however, no matter how different the end results may be, there is a 'common interest', in that each group has started out from the same basic stimulus.

See also 1.56 and 1.57 Childhood memories (1 and 2), 5.1 AC-RONYMICS, 6.4 Faces and places, 6.9 Maps, 7.2 The time has come.

4.7 It means a lot to me

What to do

Each student is asked to bring one object to class of which he or she is especially fond, or which means a lot to him or her (e.g. a photograph, an ornament, an old theatre programme, a postcard, a coin, etc.).

In groups of four, the students tell each other about their objects and what their special significance is.

Each group then uses the objects as the basis for a short dramatization which involves them all, and all their important associations.

Remarks

Level: elementary upwards.

This can be a very powerful exercise if the objects brought in are truly significant for those who bring them. To quote Ernst Becker, 'everyone wishes to be an object of primary interest in a world of meaningful action', and this provides a perfect activity for accommodating both these human needs.

As a preliminary to this exercise – and a means of focusing attention – one can also ask the students to conceal their objects. The group then has a limited amount of time (about six minutes) to guess what each person's object is.

Another idea for warming up is to ask the students to work in shifting pairs, i.e. each moves on to another partner when he or she so wishes. Before beginning, the students are told to think of any momentous *letter* they have received: they should try to recall details such as how long ago it was, whether it was expected or unexpected, what the envelope looked like, and – of course! – what the contents were. In pairs, they then discuss their recollections.

See also 1.56 and 1.57 Childhood memories (1 and 2), 2.13 From my album, 3.16 High point.

4.8   Fashion show

What to do

The students work in groups of three or four. The task is for each group to present a fashion show for another group. This involves describing in as vivid a way as possible the *actual* clothes being worn by group members. (Some groups may prefer to nominate one person as the presenter, who therefore does not appear as a model in the show.) After careful preparation, the groups present their shows to each other.

Remarks

Level: elementary to intermediate upwards.

It is important to leave groups sufficient time to prepare the verbal presentation (fifteen minutes minimum), as this usually needs to be written out.

This is an exercise which can be done at many levels of sophistication. Clearly, it could be done as merely a flat, factual description, but if the groups are given time for thoughtful presentation they will come to see the openings for fantasy and irony. As a preliminary exercise, in order to get thoughts running along the right lines, it is worth asking the class as a whole to suggest expressions they would expect to encounter in a typical fashion report ('the casual look', 'a graceful, kimono-style shift', 'for the man-on-the-move', 'chic, but not fussy' etc.). An excellent warming-up exercise is 2.4 Back-to-back.

See also 3.4 What am I wearing?, 3.21 Bringing a picture to life, 4.9 Statues.

4.9   Statues

What to do

a)   In pairs, one person 'sculpts' the other. Before beginning, the 'statue' and the 'sculptor' should decide *where* the statue is going to be placed – in a courtyard, on a mountain, on a staircase, etc. The human material with which the sculptor works is malleable at first, but gradually it stiffens into position. The statue has the right to offer suggestions and make complaints about the position in which he or she is being sculpted. Once the statues are completed, the sculptors step back, then go round to inspect the other statues. They should talk to the statues, try to find out what (if anything) they represent, what they feel about their life, what they see every day etc.

b) Each sculptor now chooses a statue other than his or her own and reshapes it according to the statue's wishes and his or her own tastes. The sculptors then return to their original statues and try to get them back into their former position.

c) Combined statues: three statues now combine to form one, through which it is possible to crawl. The sculptors are absorbed into the statue. Each statue is allowed to dissolve and crawl through the others before re-forming.

Remarks

Level: elementary upwards.

Before beginning this exercise, the students could try a warming-up exercise in which everyone is asked to take up the attitude of a well-known piece of sculpture. This position should be held until fatigue sets in. The reasons for fatigue should be discussed. Later, in the exercise itself, the statue should try to think of itself as a living being, able to observe all that goes on around it. If the students become involved in stage (a), the discussion should be allowed to continue for as long as the statues can hold their positions.

A similar exercise could be done with tailor's/shop-window dummies instead of statues.

See also 1.14 Eels in the grotto, 3.20 Becoming a picture, 3.24 Tableaux, 4.5 Cork, stone and wood.

4.10   Rules of the game

What to do

This exercise should be done in small groups of two or four (even numbers being preferable). Each pair is asked to invent a new ball game. The only restriction is that it should be an entirely new game, with its own rules. As the players will be expected to *play* their own game, it is advisable to tell the pairs not to sit down while working out the rules. The rules should be *written down* clearly so that they can be understood by anyone else.

There are two ways of continuing the exercise:

a) When one pair is ready, it demonstrates its game to another pair; the observers try to work out the rules by watching the mimed game. The players can answer any questions, but explanations should be given with the body rather than with words. The written rules serve for final reference.

b) Two pairs exchange the rules of their games; each now tries to play the other's game by following the written rules; when ready, they 'perform' for each other. The inventors of the game comment on the way it is played, and the players comment on any weaknesses in the rules, or points that might be improved.

(See below for examples of games invented during drama sessions.)

Remarks

Level: elementary to intermediate upwards.

A good balance is struck here between speech and movement. It will be noticed, also, that the obligation to formulate the rules *in writing* in fact ensures greater precision of movement in the game itself. If the rules are not written down, the players tend to be satisfied with crude action. Although it is in fact difficult to formulate rules in a foreign language, it should be remembered that here the players have *themselves* invented the rules, and therefore control the language in which they are expressed.

It helps to remind players that the ball can be any size, any shape, and made of any material.

See also 1.16 Catch!, 1.17 Tug-o'-war, 1.28 Slow motion, 5.9 The Devil's dictionary, 6.2 Boxed-in, section 8 A day's work.

EXAMPLES OF GAMES INVENTED

1 *Mouthball*
   a) A paper ball must be used.
   b) One player throws the paper ball in the direction of the other two players, who must try to catch it in their mouths without touching one another and by moving only their heads.
   c) Swallowing the ball is forbidden. Any player who does so will be disqualified.

2 *Chairball*
   Two players; two goals
   a) Each player has two chairs with which he may move.
   b) Feet may not be placed on the ground.
   c) The aim is to get the ball under the opponent's goal-chair.
   d) The goal can be moved.
   e) Players in the same team may change chairs.

3 *The Burning Ball*
   a) Players stand upright in a circle.
   b) One begins the game, by throwing the ball to another.

c) The player must send the ball on to another player by touching it only with his or her hands, and without holding it. The ball must not touch any other part of the body.

d) If the ball falls to the ground, it goes back to the thrower.

e) If the ball touches any player, the thrower shouts 'Stop', and the player concerned drops out.

4.11 Group story

What to do

The students work in groups of four. Each is given three words at an appropriate level (taken, perhaps, from the *Cambridge English Lexicon*). Each student should have one noun, one verb, and one adjective or adverb. The words should be chosen and distributed at random.

Each group then shares its words, with all members helping each other over meanings if necessary. The group's words should then be built into a coherent story line. The story is then told to another group.

Alternatively, the group works out a story line, then acts out the story to another group. This can be done in mime, in which case the other group has to derive the original words from the action.

Remarks

Level: intermediate upwards.

Two points which recur throughout the book are worth stressing here:

a) working with only minimal material, students often produce highly imaginative and unexpected results;

b) in exercises such as this, it should be remembered that although the basic material may be slender, the language it will give rise to – particularly in discussing how it could be developed – will be both rich and useful.

See also 4.6 Something in common (2), 5.10 Random dictionary, 5.15 Group poem.

4.12 Strange news

What to do

This exercise should be done in groups of two or three. Each group is given a number of newspaper headlines or parts of headlines. Their task is to fit the headlines together so as to make a short coherent passage. In order to link the headlines, they may add not more than five words for the whole passage. For example, FREAK WAVE HITS SEASIDE RESORT. 'NO NEED FOR CONCERN' SAYS PRIME MINISTER but CHURCH COUNCIL IN BRIGHTON DISTURBED by REPORTS OF UNIDENTIFIED FLYING OBJECTS above THE TROUBLED WATERS OF THE CHANNEL.

Alternatively, after the groups have been working for about five minutes, they can be given two extra headlines each. These new headlines may be either used or exchanged. In order to exchange a headline, one member of the group must offer it to another in return for a different headline.

When all the passages are ready, the results are inspected.

Alternatively, one group mimes to another the essence of its short news piece. The observers will attempt to reconstruct the headlines from the mime. (For examples of headlines, see 3.5 Split headlines.)

Remarks

Level: intermediate upwards.

This exercise is particularly useful for those who have only a limited command of the language. Although they will be working with 'fixed phrases', the result they produce will be quite unpredictable.

The mime, if attempted, requires great patience. It is not, however, as difficult as it may seem. Students who have already been exposed to 3.18 The hotel receptionist will be familiar with the techniques needed for 'helping' the observers.

See also 3.5 Split headlines, 3.6 Split exchanges, 3.8 Jumbled stories, 4.13 Starting from scratch, 5.10 Random dictionary, 7.3 Colourful ideas.

4.13 **Starting from scratch** (mime sketches based on pictures, sounds, and newspaper cuttings)

What to do

Below are very brief outlines of certain approaches to mime. These may be used either as warming-up exercises for longer activities (some suggestions are given in brackets) or as full-length activities in themselves.

1 The class is divided into four groups. Each group should decide on

an *object* to mime. One member of each group then goes to another group and mimes this object until they guess what it is. He or she now remains with this group until the end.

Next, each group decides on an *action* to mime. Again, one member of each group goes to another group and mimes the action.

Finally, each group decides upon a *character* to mime. As before, one member moves on to mime the character to another group.

Each group has now 'collected' two objects, two actions, and two characters (i.e. the ones they originally thought of and the ones they were shown by others). The groups now work out a short sketch involving their two objects, actions, and characters. The sketches may be mimed with or without words. (*See also* 4.7 It means a lot to me.)

2 The class is divided into groups of five. Each group is given the picture of an unknown person (*see* 3.12 Interviews (2)), and should work out as much detailed information as possible about the person. One member of the group notes down this information. The groups then pass their pictures to other groups and do the same thing with the picture they receive. When each group has discussed *three* characters in detail, they should work out a brief sketch involving them. (*See also* 3.21 Bringing a picture to life, 3.16 High point, 4.8 Fashion show.)

3 The class is divided into groups of five. Each student makes a brief note of what he or she hears when a tape-recording of four isolated sounds is played (e.g. a dog barking, a glass breaking, footsteps, a heavy splash). The groups now have to combine these sounds into a brief sketch suggesting how they are related. (*See also* 3.22 Picture sets, and for further ideas Maley and Duff: *Sounds interesting* and *Sounds intriguing* – see Bibliography.)

4 Two or three newspapers are torn up at random into pieces about 14 cm x 15 cm. The class is divided into groups of five, and each group is given three or four pieces. They can select any *three* items around which to construct a short sketch – an 'item' may be a headline, part of an advertisement, a single word, or a sentence from an article. (*See also* 3.5 Split headlines, 3.8 Jumbled stories, 4.12 Strange news, 5.7 Odd news, 5.10 Random dictionary.)

Remarks

Level: elementary to intermediate upwards.

These activities are essentially the same, in that they take a number of random stimuli which have to be incorporated into a coherent dramatized story line. Once again, the discussion which precedes and accompanies these activities is at least as important as the execution of the ideas, for it is in the discussion that the real conditions for interaction are created.

4.14 **Amazimbi** (creating a new language)

What to do

The class is divided into groups of four. Each group has to make up five phrases or sentences in a totally unknown language. None of the words used should even resemble words from known languages. Each phrase or sentence should have a demonstrable meaning, but the five phrases need not be linked logically. The organizer should decide whether to explain the purpose of the exercise at this stage, or only once the phrases have been created.

At least twelve minutes should be allowed for preparation. Each member of the group must master and understand the five utterances in the group's language. The group must agree on pronunciation. At the end of the preparation time, the groups split up. Each person works with someone from another group. They take it in turns to teach the other their five utterances. The 'teacher' may use only gestures and the words of the new language. The 'learner' may ask questions and put forward suggestions as to what he or she thinks the meaning is. The 'teacher' will indicate, by word or gesture, whether the 'learner' is right or wrong. Once the utterance has been understood, it should be repeated to get the right pronunciation. After ten minutes, the roles are switched, and the 'teacher' becomes the 'learner'.

An example of five utterances in the new language would be:
Amazimbi — Sit down, take a seat
Mi iizim kula? — How do you feel?
Kula hamningi klapa? — Do you eat a lot?
Neikko — Yes; *Kaiiko* – No
Amazembi — Get up

Remarks

Level: elementary to intermediate upwards.

After a certain initial reticence, even embarrassment, the groups will begin to lose their self-consciousness. Paradoxically, this exercise, which concerns some of the most important problems in language learning, often proves most difficult to the linguistically talented! As 'teachers' they become impatient, as 'learners' recalcitrant. By the end of the exercise, however, it is usually clear to everyone how much patience and ingenuity are required to convey the meaning of unknown words.

A great deal of energy goes into the creation of these new languages. It is advisable, therefore, to allow for a winding-down stage. Fifteen to twenty minutes can be allowed for the reciprocal teaching. After this, it is worth holding an informal round-up session. This can begin with each group saying its five utterances in chorus, the others merely listening. Then each person in the room says one utterance that he or she has learnt and understood. Finally, each group can explain some of the secrets of its language, e.g. '*Ama-* is an imperative form', '*Kula* is the polite form for "you"', '*-ko* at the end of a word signifies definitiveness', etc.

If the exercise is enjoyed, it is worth letting it continue on another occasion. Ways of following this up include:

a) asking each group to work out a *chant* and *dance* using any of their utterances, or inventing a new one;

b) asking each group to perform a short dramatized version of a folk legend in their new culture. They may invent new phrases for their piece, but these should be explained before the legend is demonstrated;

c) giving all groups a set of utterances in a known language (French, English, Spanish, etc.) and asking them to find their own 'phrase-book' equivalents for these.

See also 5.4 Off the-cuff, 5.9 The Devil's dictionary, 5.10 Random dictionary, 5.17 Cadavre exquis, 7.2 The time has come, 7.7 Computer poems.

4.15   Patent pending

What to do

Material needed: sketching paper and felt pens. This exercise can be done individually or in pairs. It will be described here for pairs.

Each pair has the same task: to conceive an instrument or appliance that they would like to patent. No restrictions need be made as to the size, cost, shape or function of this instrument. It may, however, be useful to remind the class as a whole of recent inventions (e.g. the alcohol-powered car engine) in order to set their minds working (see below for examples of recent inventions). They should also be encouraged to invent something they genuinely consider useful (e.g. a pocket Muzak neutralizer, which would block out the sound of music in public buildings for those who prefer silence!).

At least ten minutes should be allowed for discussion, so that several ideas can be talked over before one is chosen. Each pair works at its own speed. Once the details have been decided on, a drawing of the appliance is made. This should be done carefully. Arrows pointing to important parts can be used, but *no words* should appear on the sketch. When the sketches are ready, one person from each pair moves to somebody else. The new partners now look at each others' sketches and try to work out what is being patented. The 'inventor' avoids telling more about his or her invention than is asked, though at the end of the exercise a full explanation may be given. Criticism, and suggestions for adaptation of the inventions should be encouraged.

Remarks

Level: intermediate upwards.

The more careful the drawings, the more interesting the discussion. The organizer may need to keep an eye on the sketches, and suggest in some cases that they be done again. (Often they are too small.) Although drawing is not in itself a 'language activity', it should not be forgotten that when two people are working on the same design, there will be almost constant discussion. It is important that the students should not feel that the time spent in drawing was wasted. Having the sketches exhibited in the room may help to improve the quality of the work.

See also 1.43 Backs, 3.15 Unknown gadgets, 4.2 Emblems, 4.3 Signs of the future.

EXAMPLES OF RECENT INVENTIONS

A new medical device developed in Norway makes it easy – and safe – to transport seriously injured accident victims or hospital patients from an ambulance to a bed, from one bed to another, or from a bed to an operating or examination table. The Paroll Roller, invented by Kjell Roisaeth, consists of a pair of boards mounted on rollers that can be strapped beneath a patient's shoulders and hips. A head support ensures that the patient's entire upper torso is immobilized during movement. The rollers slide easily on a second pair of boards that can be placed on a bed or table as runners when positioning the patient in a new location. Finally, there is a rod that connects to the strapped-on boards so that the immobilized patient can be turned over on his back or stomach during examinations. (*Newsweek,* 17 August 1981)

Want an alibi? The 'Alibi Tape' could be just the thing if you are planning the perfect crime, or just a dirty weekend.

It is a cassette which supplies 14 different backgrounds to authenticate any of 14 different lies you care to tell over the telephone.

'Most of our customers are having a love affair on the side, and need to convince their wives that they're tied up on business,' says Takao Takeuchi, whose firm is marketing the tape... The cassette is also proving popular with office girls who are under strict parental orders to be home by a certain hour. 'Mum, I'm going to be a bit late – I'm with some of the girls from the office drinking a cup of coffee,' says our demure Miss, selecting the 'coffee shop' soundtrack (clatter of cups, murmur of earnest conversation) as her boyfriend nuzzles up to her in one of Japan's ubiquitous 'love hotels'.

(*The Sunday Times*, 16 August 1981)

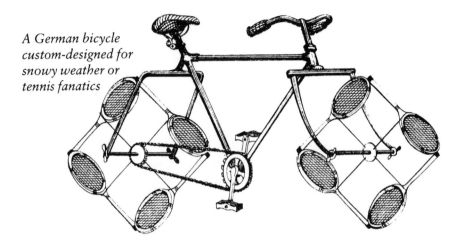

A German bicycle custom-designed for snowy weather or tennis fanatics

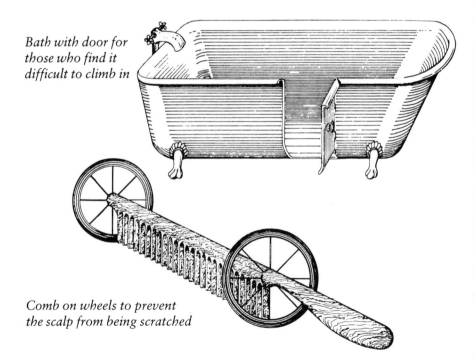

Bath with door for those who find it difficult to climb in

Comb on wheels to prevent the scalp from being scratched

4.16   Making a machine

What to do

This is an extremely rich exercise, and one which can be done in many different ways. As set out below, it would take between forty-five minutes and an hour. The various stages, however, may be approached separately.

1 WARMING UP

   a) The whole class together tries out certain machine movements, e.g. vertical movement (a pump), horizontal movement (a conveyer belt), spiral movement (an oil drill), circular movement (a fan) etc. The organizer suggests the machine he or she has in mind, and each member of the group performs the appropriate movements independently. (approx. five mins)
   b) *Teaching a Martian to breathe, walk, eat, sleep.* Students work in pairs. One is a Martian, the other an 'earthling'. The exercise begins with the Martian lying as a helpless lump on the ground (his space-ship having crashed). The earthling finds him. Slowly, he teaches the Martian to breathe. He must make his partner fill his lungs and empty them several times, etc. He then teaches him to walk. They walk home. At home, he shows the Martian how to eat with a knife and fork, how to sit 'properly', etc. Finally, he puts the space visitor to bed. (approx. ten mins)

2 THE MACHINE

   Students work in groups of four or five. The instructions are: 'Each group is to create a machine that is not yet known on earth. A machine of the year 2500. It may, of course, be a fantasy machine, *but* it must operate. Each member of the group is a functioning part of the machine. Your machine will be demonstrated at the 1st Interstellar Industrial Fair. You will be competing against industrialists from other planets and from Earth. One person in the group, therefore, should be prepared to present the machine at the Fair, to demonstrate how it functions and explain its advantages. All publicity tricks are permitted, e.g. the machine can sing its own slogans, etc.' (approx. fifteen to twenty mins)

3 THE DEMONSTRATION

   The machines are presented individually to the whole class. During the demonstration, the rest of the class act as Martian spectators. The demonstrator should be prepared to answer any queries concerning the functioning of his or her group's machine.

Remarks

Level: elementary to intermediate upwards.

This exercise is usually enjoyed, because it not only offers a good balance between intellectual and physical activity, but also provides an outlet for group inventiveness. The problem of self-consciousness, which so often mars demonstrations in front of the whole group, is rarely encountered because most people are relaxed by the physical effort of the preparations.

Note: experience shows that it is unwise to prepare the machine sitting down. The longer people sit, the more sedentary their ideas become. Organizers who do not like being directive might take the precaution of removing all chairs before beginning.

The machines may need to be reminded that this is not a silent mime exercise. All sounds, words, percussions and explosions are permitted.

See also 1.7 Sounds with the right shape, 1.33 Don't break it!, 1.38 Becoming a musical instrument, 2.18 Lost memory, 3.21 Bringing a picture to life, 4.8 Fashion show.

4.17 People, places, problems and things

What to do

a) Material needed: separate slips of paper for *themes* and *scenes*, e.g.

Theme	Scene
Crime doesn't pay	on a picnic
Nobody loves me	at a supermarket
You get what you deserve	in an airport
Live now, pay later	on a building site
Men/women are all the same	in the British Museum
They're always...	at a transport cafe

The theme slips are placed in one box, the scene slips in another.

The class is divided into groups of five. A representative from each group comes to take one slip from each box. The groups then have to prepare a short sketch based on the theme and the scene which they have drawn (e.g. Nobody loves me + in the British Museum). They will of course need to invent the characters who will be involved in the incident. When the sketch is ready, it should be performed for another group, who comment and criticize.

b) Material needed: separate slips of paper for a *person*, a *place*, the *time* and the *weather*, e.g.

Person	Place	Time	Weather
a bus-conductor	a ferry	midnight	showery
a hijacker	a tea-room	after lunch	foggy
a tramp	a forest	dawn	a drought
a bank-manager	a beach	1914	a gale
a pop-star	an ice-cream factory	21.20	humid

The slips are put into four separate boxes. The class is divided into a convenient number of groups (four or five per group). A representative of each group comes and takes one slip from each box, except the *person* box, from which he or she takes three slips. The groups then have to construct a short sketch using the information on the slips. When ready, they act out their sketch for other groups. Before commenting and criticizing, the observer group should try to establish *precisely* who the characters in the sketch were.

Remarks

Level: intermediate upwards.

Once again, the slips of paper simply offer groups a starting-point for the exercise of their own imagination. The need to come to an agreement on a story line and the allotting of roles, and to offer comment and criticism, leads again to the production of language in authentic circumstances.

See also 3.10 One-word dialogues, 3.14 Inkblots, 4.1 The all-purpose sock, 4.6 Something in common (2), 6.4 Faces and places.

4.18 **Act Three** (an extension of Kim's game)

What to do

In 2.17 Kim's game, various objects were placed on a table, and the students had to remember them. Here, the same objects are used, but more than half of them are removed from the table, leaving about six or seven objects to be used. The students are told that these objects are all closely linked in a three-act play. Two acts of the play have already been performed, the third is about to begin.

In groups of four, the students now work out: (a) what the play has been about up till now, (b) what the last act will be about. For (a) they can prepare a brief description, for (b) they prepare a sketch of part of the last act (not necessarily the end) to be acted out. When groups are ready, they should find another group to perform for. Comment and comparison follows the two sketches.

Clearly, the direction of the play can be to some extent influenced by the selection of objects. For instance, a rose, a letter, a knife, a lady's glove, a photograph of a child, and an empty glass will suggest one kind of play, whereas an electric torch, a pair of spectacles, a pocket Russian–English dictionary, a screwdriver, a railway ticket and a foreign banknote will suggest quite another.

As this is an exercise which requires considerable time for development, we suggest that the work be spread over two sessions:

session 1 – Kim's game; the groups decide on their stories;
session 2 – groups work out details of action and prepare Act Three; performance for other groups and discussion.

Remarks

Level: intermediate to advanced.

This activity demands sustained effort. Here the interaction is taking place fully, not only in discussion and decision-making but also in the performance itself.

See also 2.12 Clues, 2.17 Kim's game, 3.25 Detective work, 7.4 Starters, 7.10 Spring fever.

4.19 **Waking dream**

What to do

The class should sit or lie in a circle, facing outwards so that nobody is looking at anyone else. The organizer begins a story (see 1.54 Directed group fantasies, for an example), which he or she cuts off at a certain – possibly climactic – moment. Members of the group then continue the story *without being called upon* at any particular moment to intervene, i.e. they speak when they like, each person taking up the thread from the last, adapting and changing the story line in whatever way he or she likes.

Remarks

Level: elementary upwards.

At the end of a long session of concentrated work, this exercise helps to calm the class. There may well be some self-conscious giggling, coughing, shuffling at the beginning; this is normal, because the class may not yet be accustomed to silence. Once this has been overcome, however, extremely interesting developments will emerge.

See also 1.53 Group dream, 1.54 Directed group fantasies.

4.20 Music pictures

What to do

Material needed: large sheets of paper to be distributed around the room, on the walls or on the floor. There should be one sheet per person, and a supply of coloured felt pens.

A piece of music – preferably not well-known – is played. Each student begins drawing to the rhythm of the music on one of the sheets of paper. The drawing is allowed to continue for up to a minute. Then the students are told to change papers. This is most easily done by getting them all to move in one direction, e.g. to the left, or anticlockwise. They now continue the drawing in front of them. Approximately every forty-five seconds they move on. After about five moves, the drawings are collected. They will not be used immediately, as they are still too fresh in the mind. At a later session, however (possibly the next day), they will be brought out again.

In the next session, the class is divided into groups of four or five. Each group is given four or five of the drawings and asked to arrange them around a specific theme suggested by the content of the pictures themselves. Thus, the pictures may all be illustrations from a book on nuclear physics, or graffiti from an underground passage, or photographs from a biology text-book, or rejected plans from an architect's office, etc. They must, however, all belong to the same context. Each group then spreads out its 'exhibition'; one member stays behind to answer questions, while the others circulate and inspect the other exhibitions.

Remarks

Level: elementary upwards.

As the first part of the exercise is entirely non-verbal, it is best done at the end of a long day. Students should be discouraged from asking *why* they are doing the exercise. They will understand when they come to see – with fresh eyes – the drawings they produced.

See also 3.22 Picture sets, 4.2 Emblems, 4.4 Potato figures, 5.14 Words for music.

4.21 Zoo story

What to do

a) The class is divided into 'animals' and 'the public'. Each person in the animal group decides on an animal that might be found in a zoo (aquarium or aviary). Each animal marks out its own 'cage-space': no physical barriers are erected. The public then visits the animals. The visitors may behave as they like, ignoring some animals, offering food to others; but they should attempt to strike up a conversation with each of the animals to find out how they feel about their caged existence.

b) *The animals' dream:* if possible, the room should be darkened for this stage of the exercise. (Music could also be used to create an atmosphere of calm.) Each member of the public should now choose one of the animals. He or she will become an animal of the same species, a free animal, who will revisit his or her captive fellow-animal in a dream. In the dream, each animal talks to the other of his or her own kind; they exchange experiences of life in captivity and life in freedom.

Remarks

Level: elementary upwards.

If this exercise is to succeed, it is important that each person involved should concentrate on 'becoming' the animal of his or her choice. Much noise and excitement will be generated in the first stage of the exercise. It is important that the atmosphere changes in the second stage. This is why we suggest darkening the room.

See also 1.55 Hunter and hunted, 1.56 and 1.57 Childhood memories (1 and 2), 3.30 Dream themes, 4.9 Statues, 7.6 What's in a name?

4.22 Dream home

What to do

a) Students work in pairs. Each pair is asked to imagine a feature for a futuristic apartment, e.g. a completely new kind of window, for instance one that can change shape without opening. Together, they should mime the functioning of this window. The pairs then exchange ideas.

b) Students work in groups of four or five. Each group is asked to

create an apartment of the future. They should concentrate specifically on replacing the following features with revolutionary ideas:
– tables and chairs
– windows
– doors
– beds
– the lighting system
They will be asked to present their new apartment at an exhibition in the year 2080. Each person in the group, then, will be expected to 'become' the furniture, while at the same time explaining how it works. Once the group is ready, it should present its new apartment to another group. The other group asks questions and offers comment.

Remarks

Level: intermediate upwards.

This exercise is similar to 4.16 Making a machine, with the difference that here the task is more complex while at the same time being somewhat easier to perform. As it is a more complex exercise, it is best not to have a presentation before the whole class since it is almost impossible to ensure that the non-performing groups concentrate sufficiently on the performers. (Those who have not yet 'performed' are interested only in putting the finishing touches to their 'act'!) While preparing their apartment, the groups should be reminded that the design will be influenced by the person who is to live there. They should, therefore, try to imagine a specific dweller and his or her needs.

See also 3.15 Unknown gadgets, 4.15 Patent pending, 4.16 Making a machine.

4.23 Masks

What to do

The class is divided into groups of six. Each group is given masks (these masks could also be made as a separate activity). The groups then prepare a mimed story around a theme – the life cycle of a man, the rise and fall of a dictator, a legend, or folk story.

When the groups are ready they put on masks and – using appropriate music if they wish – take it in turns to act out their mime. The other groups try to identify the theme from the mime, and offer comment and criticism.

Remarks

Level: elementary upwards.

The use of masks is an extremely powerful and effective theatrical device. It also has the advantage for shyer students of allowing them to hide their nervousness. The guessing and comment at the end of each group's mime leads to very lively genuine conversation.

See also 3.8 Jumbled stories, 3.30 Dream themes, 4.13 Starting from scratch, 4.14 Amazimbi.

4.24 Visual consequences

What to do

The students work in groups of five. Each person has a sheet of paper. Everyone is instructed to draw a head at the top of the paper, including the beginnings of the neck (it may be human, animal or fantastic). The sheets of paper are then folded so that the head is not visible, and passed on to the next person in the group. Everyone then draws the top half of the creature (with arms, wings, or other appendages). Sheets of paper are passed on again. The same procedure is followed for the trunk, legs, and lower limbs. At the end, everyone unfolds his or her sheet of paper and compares it with those of others in the group. The result will be five 'creatures', rather like the example below.

The group is now asked to discuss these five creatures, to assign them names, and to invent a character – even a history – for each of them.

A dramatization is then worked out involving the five creatures, and acted by the group for another group.

Remarks

Level: elementary upwards.

There is enormous intrinsic interest in seeing what the creatures turn out to be like, and the resulting dramatizations are usually highly inventive.

See also 3.14 Inkblots, 4.6 Something in common (2), 5.15 Group poem, 7.3 Colourful ideas.

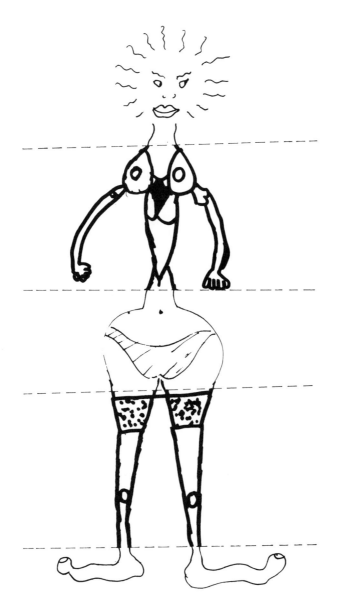

Example of a creature drawn by a group

4.25 Street demonstration

What to do

Groups of four or five are formed. Each group is asked to prepare itself for a street demonstration. They should – obviously – decide *what* they are demonstrating about, what their grievances are, whose sympathy or attention they wish to attract, how angry they are, etc. The groups must prepare large banners with slogans, and can, if they wish, produce leaflets to be distributed to the crowd. Each group will also be expected to make a speech, which may be either prepared or off-the-cuff, delivered by one person or by the group as a whole.

Each group then demonstrates, using the other groups as the crowd. The crowd should heckle, barrack and interrupt, ask questions or 'offer advice'.

Remarks

Level: intermediate upwards.

This is an exercise for 'letting off steam' and can – when it goes well – become difficult to control. If it is to succeed, there will inevitably be noise, and any attempt to cut down on the noise level is likely to destroy the vitality of the demonstration. It is, therefore, probably best to hold it outside, or in a large empty hall, e.g. a gymnasium.

It should be added, however, that the groups themselves will act as noise-controllers, because at some stage in each demonstration a speech will be made which must somehow be heard.

For those who wish for any reason to avoid the 'live' demonstration, it is possible to tame the exercise by asking the groups to prepare their slogans and handouts before meeting with just *one* other group to whom they try to *explain* their point of view.

See also 4.2 Emblems, 4.8 Fashion show, 4.16 Making a machine, 5.2 Listen to me!, 7.2 The time has come.

5 Word-play

5.1 ACRONYMICS

What to do

The class divides into pairs. Each pair draws up a list of acronyms (the initial letters of a body, movement or association, e.g. OPEC, NATO, UNESCO). These may be real or fictitious. Real acronyms can easily be found in any dictionary, under 'Common abbreviations'.

Each pair now works out a *new* meaning for the letters it has chosen. For instance: WHO = White House Occupant; EEC = the Extroverts and Eccentrics Club. Common abbreviations, such as RSVP and PTO, may also be used.

Not more than five to eight minutes should be allowed for preparation. Each pair then works with another pair. They exchange their lists of abbreviations, and each tries to work out, by questioning, the meaning of the letters. Clues may, of course, be offered.

Remarks

Level: intermediate to advanced.

In our own language, most acronyms are familiar, and if they are not, we can usually guess at their meaning. In a foreign language, however, they may for a long time remain mysterious – as anyone who has tried to look up telephone numbers (e.g. for railway information) in a foreign directory will know.

The purpose here is not to teach acronyms, but to use them, playfully, as a warming-up exercise to set the tongue moving. As the 'right' answer is never needed, there is no danger of anyone being handicapped by their own 'ignorance'.

Although the exercise does not *directly* teach anything, it does *indirectly* help to practise something all too often forgotten – word order. Here, the simple framework of a few letters offers the chance to *predict* an order of words which will almost certainly reflect a deeper pattern in the language.

See also 3.21 Bringing a picture to life.

5.2 Listen to me!

What to do

a) Six students are chosen. One is asked to stand aside. Each of the others is given a slip of paper with a sentence or two reflecting his or her need or preoccupation, e.g. 'I'm looking for the Post Office', 'Can you change a five-pound note for me?', 'My car's broken down, please help me push it'.

First one person goes up to the student standing aside and starts up a conversation based on his or her sentence. As soon as the dialogue is going, a second student joins them and tries to get the other two to take notice of *his* or *her* need. When these three are talking, another student joins in, then another, and another. Each student should stick to *his* or *her* message and insist on putting it over. Everyone should *keep talking*.

b) Once the whole class has seen how the activity works, the students are divided into groups of six. Each group is given similar slips of paper. Not more than five minutes are allowed for the activity to develop as in (a) above.

Remarks

Level: elementary upwards.

Although short, this is more than just a warming-up exercise.

If it is to work successfully, strict control will need to be kept both over the time limit and over the noise level! In spite of the obvious difficulties, however, it is worth trying out for two reasons:

1 The students are obliged to keep talking against the flow of other people's talk, and thus can develop their confidence in being able to *keep going* in the foreign language (particularly since their mistakes are unlikely to be heard!).

2 The messages can be expressed in a variety of ways, for example:
Can you change a five-pound note for me?
Has anyone got change for a five-pound note?
I need change for five pounds.
Who can change a five-pound note for me?

Before starting the activity, the students could be asked to jot down two or three ways of saying their message. If they wish, they can refer to these notes while talking.

Here are some suggestions for the kind of sentences that might be used in this exercise:
− Does this wallet belong to anyone? I found it on the floor.
− Can you help me open my umbrella? It's stuck.

– Who won the match this afternoon?
– Repent! The end of the world is at hand!
– How do you say 'backfire' in Portuguese?
– Would you mind moving your car – it's blocking the way!
– I like your shoes. Where did you get them?
– You're wanted on the phone, at least I think it's you.
– I'm conducting a survey. Could you tell me which bus route you use and how often you travel?

See also 1.41 Gift of the gab, 3.6 Split exchanges, 3.18 The hotel receptionist, 5.4 Off the cuff, 5.5 Persuasion, 5.6 Does the humming-bird fly backwards?

5.3 Word for word

What to do

The students sit in a big circle. One person starts off by saying a word, e.g *black*. The next person on the right has to say a word which 'goes with' this word, e.g. *sheep*. The next person continues in the same way, e.g. *wool*, etc. Here is an example of such a series:
Book – worm – earth – sky – blue – sea – fish – swim – sink – dishes – food – supermarket – shoplifting – detective ...

From here, if one wishes, one may lead straight into what John C. Maher has described as 'The rhyming verse game'. The group is asked to think of words with the same sound (this may be an *internal* sound, like the *o* in the examples below – but it could also be a rhyme), e.g. *go, slow, soak, show, home, told*. Each word is written on a slip of paper, and the slips are mixed. Each person then draws two slips of paper, which he or she uses to write a two-line rhyming verse, e.g.

She said 'Absolutely no!'   I don't like mowing,
So I couldn't go.   But the grass keeps on growing!

Remarks

Level: elementary to intermediate upwards.

The first exercise is the equivalent in words of the non-verbal (physical) warming-up exercises, and works well at all levels. The second is an optional follow-on. Both will waken the mind for more difficult tasks, and neither need take more than a few minutes.

See also 7.5 Alphabet poems, 7.7 Computer poems.

5.4 Off the cuff

What to do

Each member of the class writes down a word – a noun – on a slip of paper. The slips of paper are then collected and mixed together. The group divides into pairs, and each person is given one slip of paper. At the signal to start, one person in each pair begins talking, *without reflection*, around the word written on the paper. The purpose is to talk coherently for two minutes without actually mentioning the word (*anaconda, igloo, vaccine*, etc.). The listener may at any time challenge the speaker by guessing what the word is. If the speaker lasts the full two minutes without being correctly challenged, he or she has 'won'.

The exercise is then repeated, this time with the other partner speaking.

Remarks

Level: intermediate upwards.

This is an exercise in quick thinking. It is not a test in mastery of the language but a means of developing the vital skill of speaking unprepared. It is important, then, that the speaker should have no time for reflection, but also that he or she should not be required to speak for too long. Hence the time limit of two minutes.

The exercise may be done on its own, as a warming-up exercise, or combined with other short exercises, such as the two which follow.

See also 3.10 One-word dialogues, 3.12 Interviews, 3.27 Conflict, 5.2 Listen to me!

5.5 Persuasion

What to do

Each person writes down a single word on a slip of paper; the slips are folded, collected, and mixed together. The class divides into pairs and each person is given a slip of paper. (If this exercise is preceded by 5.4 Off the cuff, the same slips of paper could be redistributed.)

The pairs now start up a free conversation, in which each partner tries to get the other to say the word written on his or her own slip of paper. That is, if A has the word *glacier* and B has the word *varnish*, A will try to get B to say *glacier* and B will try to get A to say *varnish*. Each therefore tries to steer the conversation in the direction he or she wants. The exercise continues until each partner has been induced to say the word of the other.

Remarks

Level: intermediate upwards.

This is an exercise in speech tactics. Both partners know what they want the other to say, but cannot get them to say it unless they are able to steer the conversation in a given direction. As both partners are using the same tactic, each will have to listen as well as speak. Since this is not a test of speed in thinking but rather of the ability to interact, no time limit need be set. Nevertheless, seven minutes is about as long as most pairs can go on without tiring. Much spin-off value comes from the discussion of what was actually said.

See also 1.41 Gift of the gab, 5.2 Listen to me!, 5.4 Off the cuff.

5.6 Does the humming-bird fly backwards?

What to do

Each member of the class is asked to write down a grammatically coherent (but not necessarily logical) phrase, no longer than five words. This may be a complete sentence or a fragment. The class should be asked to do this as quickly as possible, i.e. 'Write down the first thing that comes to your mind, even if it does sound strange.'

The slips of paper are collected, mixed, then distributed to the class. The students form pairs. Each pair begins a free conversation, in which the partners both try to insert the five words on their slip of paper into the conversation without being challenged. If at any stage in the conversation one partner thinks that the other has introduced his or her phrase, the partner may be challenged. If the challenge is wrong, the conversation goes on.

Remarks

Level: advanced.

This is the last in a trio of closely related exercises. Here, the skill of 'thinking on your feet', which was the focus in 5.4 Off the cuff, will again be used. So too will be ability to interact, which was the focus in 5.5 Persuasion. Each partner will try to engross the other so much in what he or she says that his or her words can be slipped in unnoticed. It often happens, for this reason, that one partner dominates throughout. This is why it is worth repeating the exercise (perhaps with different partners each time) until the class realizes of its own accord that there must be 'give-and-take' for the exercise to work. They will also gradually realize that seemingly odd sets of words, such as 'Does the humming-bird fly backwards?', are more challenging – and rewarding – to work on than colourless statements, such as 'I don't like brown bread'.

See also 1.41 Gift of the gab, 1.42 My word!, 3.5 Split headlines, 3.6 Split exchanges, 4.12 Strange news.

5.7 Odd news

What to do

Material needed: the material used can be taken either from news broadcasts or from newspapers. If the radio is used, fragments of sentences are chosen at random from different broadcasts; if newspapers are used, single lines (maximum ten words) are taken from different articles. For instance, the following fragments were taken from BBC broadcasts:

- ...we taught her to use the cat-door; we didn't teach her to beg...
- Mrs Mackintosh, thank you very much for your question...
- It was the point of goodbye. How could she say goodbye?
- ...sitting down is one thing, remaining seated is another.
- ...fishing rights, oil prices, and the problem of ...

(See below for further suggestions.)

Groups of three or four are formed. Each group is given the same set of fragments (about six): these can be either written out or read aloud. Their task is to link the fragments into a coherent piece. The fragments may be used in any order, but the wording itself cannot be changed. No more than five words can be used for the linking passages between the fragments, but the groups should be encouraged to use as few words as possible. Once a group has completed its odd-news story, each member notes down the story and then goes to someone from another group to compare versions. Each person should try to exchange stories with as many people as possible.

A variant of the exercise is to distribute different sets of news fragments to the groups. Once they have worked out their stories, they should exchange their original fragments with another group. The groups now work out a coherent piece from the second set of fragments. When they have finished, they join the group with whom the exchange was made and compare what each has done with the other's material.

Remarks

Level: intermediate upwards.

It is extremely important that the groups should not be too large (three is the ideal number), as there must be opportunity for free exchange of ideas. It is also important that plenty of time be allowed for the comparison, as this is when the groups find out how *differently* they have reacted to the same material. In many of the other exercises in this book, it is precisely this difference in interpretation of the same material or the same instructions that provides the stimulus for natural discussion.

Although this is essentially a 'language' activity, it can easily be transformed into a dramatic activity by asking the groups to *mime* their news pieces. The others would then try to work out the content, if not the actual wording, of the various fragments and the meaning of the whole.

See also 3.5 Split headlines, 4.12 Strange news, 7.2 The time has come, 7.3 Colourful ideas.

EXAMPLES OF FRAGMENTS OF NEWS

...this is what I was really getting at...
...John Wesley, no. *Charles* Wesley, yes!...
...whose operation, she claims, left her navel 2 inches off-centre...
...well, it looks like a pleasant afternoon, with light breezes...
...my own cat talks to me in the evenings...
...force 5, Scilly Isles, fair to promising, with light...
...against what was seen as interference from Brussels...
...and suddenly they have a pet: a cat, a horse, a dog, a donkey...
...because Robert comes before Ronald...
...about 40 ft: it's a very considerable earthwork, and you usually find these banks around medieval villages...
...Wot d'you want to do a thing like that for? You frightened the life out of 'im!...
...She tossed her yellow-ribboned, plaited hair behind her...
...produce 60% of the bread eaten in England...
...Shell lost ten, moving down to 478; ICI plunged 10 pence to 321...
...bananas or potato-crisps. They didn't even know how to peel an orange...
...planning to paddle across the Channel five feet above the sea...
...What happens in this story? Well, there's this magpie...
...John, whose hungry mouth is pressed against *whose* sweet-flowing breast?...

5.8 News poems

What to do

Material needed: a collection of newspaper headlines (for examples, see 3.5 Split headlines).

The students work in groups of three. Each group is given about ten headlines, which must be arranged to form a poem of not more than six lines (some headlines, therefore, may be discarded). The poem need not rhyme, but it should have a consistent *rhythm*.

Once the groups have begun work, i.e. after about seven minutes, they can be told that they may, if they wish, exchange two of their headlines with other groups.

Not more than ten minutes should be allowed for the composition of the poem.

When the groups are ready, they recite or perform their poems to the other groups. If they wish, they may sing them or present them in a specific manner, e.g. as TV commercials.

Remarks

Level: intermediate to advanced.

In many of the drama activities, the students are being encouraged to look at language with fresh eyes and to forget the customary associations that accrete around words. Here – as in many of the activities in this section – the students are being encouraged to see familiar words in an unfamiliar context. In principle, nothing could seem further apart than the language of newspaper headlines and the language of verse. But the object of the exercise is not to produce great verse; it is, rather, to show – as in 3.2 Things aren't what they seem to be – how fresh life can be given to the familiar. The exercise is likely to work better with advanced students, and should not be attempted before members of the class are at ease with each other.

See also 3.11 Dialogue interpretation, 4.12 Strange news, 5.7 Odd news, 5.10 Random dictionary, 5.11 The oracle, 5.13 As mixed as a metaphor, 7.2 The time has come.

EXAMPLE OF A NEWS POEM

This poem was composed from the headlines given in 3.5 Split headlines.

Britons still look abroad for their silver lining

Huge void found in universe
Markets get world wide wobbles

Money supply down sharply in US
North Americans, too, have their tensions
Is London choking to death?

Richer or poorer – till tax do us part
Uphill battle. A lifetime on the dole
Pickpockets getting rich at Heathrow
   Nasty for you and me
   Nice for industry

Britons know little about sea food
Our spy story is gagged
Who is to blame and what should be done?
Stay in bed and call the police
Can this plan save Venice?

5.9   The Devil's dictionary

What to do

Material needed: a list of six to ten words, some of which are 'real' words that can be found in the dictionary, others invented words. The principle of selection is that the 'real' words should sound unfamiliar and the invented words familiar. (See below for examples.)

The words are read out, spelt out if necessary, and the students note them down. Working in pairs, they try to devise dictionary-style definitions for as many words as possible. Allow ten to fifteen minutes for this. A round-up session is then held. It usually proves best not to ask each pair for its definitions, but instead to read out the words on the list and call for proposed definitions. This encourages pairs who may have been reticent about their ideas to come forward.

Remarks

Level: intermediate to advanced.

It must be stressed from the start that this is *not* a general knowledge test and that nobody is expected to *know* the definition of any of the words. It need not be stated – but it should be implicitly understood – that the purpose of the exercise is to free the imagination not to shackle it. (And, incidentally, to remind students that the dictionary is an aid not a Bible!)

Although this would seem to be an exercise concerned with the written word, its real value lies in the discussion it sparks off: in order to arrive at a definition, the students will have to think aloud and react to each other's suggestions.

The title of this exercise is taken from Ambrose Bierce's book *The*

Devil's Dictionary, in which ideas for a different approach to this exercise may be found.

See also 4.10 Rules of the game, 4.14 Amazimbi, 4.15 Patent pending, 6.2 Boxed-in.

EXAMPLES OF WORDS AND DEFINITIONS

gramble
shagreen
quark
shard
multigonal
velotic
pylonitis
dowlish

gramble: parasitic creeper, derived from a cross between the grape-vine and the bramble; fashionable sport: leisurely walk punctuated by pauses for strenuous all-in wrestling; verb, describing the speech of an ill-tempered and long-winded speaker.

pylonitis: rare disease, afflicting especially the joints of metal constructions supporting electricity-bearing cables; term used in the science of behaviourism to describe tendency towards exaggeration.

dowlish: adj., fixed, penetrating gaze, reminiscent of the downy owl; coastal resort in Devon.

For further examples see Paul Jennings: *The Book of Nonsense* (see Bibliography).

5.10   Random dictionary

What to do

Material needed: an English monolingual dictionary (e.g. *Oxford Advanced Learner's Dictionary of Current English,* or *Longman Dictionary of Contemporary English*). The organizer asks the students to call out any number which falls between the first and last page (e.g. 251). He or she turns to the page named, then asks for any number between 1 and 20 (e.g. 15). He or she now looks up the fifteenth headword on the page. If this turns out to be a function word (e.g. a preposition), the next content word on the page (preferably a noun or a verb) is taken. The students write this word down. The procedure is then repeated five times. All students should now have five words chosen at random from the dictionary.

They now form groups of four. Each group is to use the words to work out a story line which can be acted as a sketch for another group.

Remarks

Level: intermediate upwards.

Those who object to the random approach in 'serious' language learning might be reminded that even so 'serious' an artist as Leonardo da Vinci claimed that he regularly drew inspiration from the random cracks, blotches and patterns on an old brick wall!

What is important here is that the students are all working from exactly *the same* material and that they are *free* to do with it what they like. It is the fact that each group begins with the same – possibly unpromising – material that ensures their later interest in each other's work, an interest that is often lacking when they have no common starting-point.

See also 3.14 Inkblots, 3.22 Picture sets, 3.26 The envelope.

5.11 The oracle

What to do

The first time this exercise is done, some preparation will be necessary. A number of 'oracular' statements which might serve as replies (if not answers) to questions are written on separate cards. This means that the formulation should be open to various interpretations, e.g. 'The cactus scorns the rose because it does not bloom in the desert', 'The grain of wheat is lost in the loaf', 'He who swims against the current remains where he is', 'Rain falls where it chooses', 'The eagle sees the mouse, the mouse does not see the eagle'.

The class is divided into groups of four or five. Each group is asked to prepare a number of questions they would like to ask the oracle. There is no restriction on what kind of questions may be asked. The questions – each on a separate slip of paper – are collected. Each group now decides on two members who will be the oracle. The oracle conceals itself in some way, e.g. behind an overcoat. The questions are now redistributed among the groups and a selection of about seven responses is handed to each oracle. Questions are now put to the oracles. The oracle answers by choosing at random one of the slips from the pile of responses. The questioners then try to interpret the response in the light of their question. If they cannot make sense of the answer, they may ask a further three clarifications of the oracle. The oracle may reply either by offering a comment of its own or by giving another response from the pile.

Remarks

Level: intermediate upwards.

As it is necessary for the oracle to be able to 'listen in' on the discussion that goes on around its response, it is advisable *not* to place a solid object (e.g. a table) between oracle and questioner. Nevertheless, it is also important – in order to maintain the illusion of a prophetic voice – that the oracle be invisible. Once the group has discovered how the exercise functions, the preparation of the oracle responses can be handed over to the groups of four or five. Note that it may be necessary to remind the class of the *kind of language* typically used here.

See also 3.6 Split exchanges, 3.13 Palmistry, the zodiac and fortune-telling, 4.2 Emblems, 7.3 Colourful ideas, and the next three exercises.

5.12 Love heals all wounds

What to do

The material needed in this exercise consists of proverbs, popular sayings, and folk wisdom. It is advisable to have a number of these ready before beginning, but they should not be introduced until the students themselves have offered suggestions. These suggestions might be, for example:
– A stitch in time saves nine.
– Too many cooks spoil the broth.
– Many hands make light work.
– Parting makes the heart grow fonder.
– Time heals all wounds.
These should either be written up as they are given or else noted down by the students. In some cases, it may be necessary to clarify the meaning.

a) Working in pairs, the students try to invent new sayings composed out of elements of the ones noted down. This may produce, for instance, 'Time makes the world go round' and 'Love heals all wounds', or 'People in glass houses should never look a gift horse in the mouth', or 'Make hay while two's company'. Or even composite proverbs, such as 'Look before you leap – still waters run deep'. After ten to fifteen minutes, the pairs should break up and each person should go round comparing his or her new proverbs with those of others. Needless to say, students must be able to explain the meaning of their proverbs. If the class is not too large, one can end with a round-up session in which each person mentions one new proverb (not his or her own) that he or she finds particularly striking.

b) As a follow-up or alternative to (a), students can be invited to *adapt* existing sayings to give them a new meaning, e.g.
 – People in glass houses shouldn't get stoned.
 – It's all mist to his grill.
 – Iron while the strike's hot.
 – A stitch in nine saves time.
This, however, is a very demanding exercise and should be reserved for advanced groups.

c) The third exercise in this series is one which links well with 5.11 The oracle, and the material produced here might well be kept for later use.
  The students are asked to *invent* their own 'folk wisdom'. This should be done in small groups of two or three. They should be encouraged to make their 'proverbs' sound as authentic as possible, e.g.
 – Plant a vine, drink wine.
 – However you have made your soup, you must eat it.
 – The stone is always colder underneath.
 – Feed the dog and it barks for you.
The pairs then break up, and each person joins up with two or three others to form a new group. In turn, members of the group read out their proverbs, which the others try to interpret. To end with, they select *one* proverb and develop a mime sketch to illustrate it. This sketch is then performed to other groups.

Remarks

Level: advanced.
  The purpose of these interrelated exercises is not to teach proverbs, but to make use of the enigmatic power of this kind of language. It should also be stressed that the language itself is often very simple, though the ideas expressed may be complex. Consequently, the discussion, particularly in (c), is most important.

See also 3.6 Split exchanges, 3.11 Dialogue interpretation, 5.11 The oracle, 5.13 As mixed as a metaphor.

5.13   As mixed as a metaphor

What to do

a)   The class is divided into two equal groups, A and B. Group A draws up a list of adjectives, group B a list of expressions beginning with 'as a ...', e.g. 'as an elephant with toothache', 'as a chimney-sweep on a tennis-court'. Group A then calls out adjectives from its list, e.g. docile, loving, reliable etc. Group B tries to find an expression from its list to make up a complete simile, e.g. 'as reliable as a Swiss banker's watch'.

b)   The class breaks up into groups of three. If numbers are uneven, pairs should be formed rather than groups of four. Each group now draws up its own list of similes – five or six will do. The list should be written out twice. One copy, the 'master', is kept by the group; the other copy, written with a space between the first and second halves of the simile, is cut down the middle. The two halves are then placed in separate piles, the first pile containing the adjectives – 'as cool as', etc. – the second pile containing the continuation, e.g. 'a tax-inspector on the telephone'. (A specimen list is given below.)

c)   Each group now takes a slip from the second pile only. The groups circulate and perform to each other. Their task is to mime each of the items on their list (e.g. 'a chimney-sweep on a tennis-court'). The group for whom they are performing must guess what they are miming. Then, together, both groups try to work out what the complete simile might be. Once they have done so, they check their ideas against the corresponding slip in the first pile (e.g. *'as smart as* a chimney-sweep on a tennis-court').

Remarks

Level: intermediate upwards.

It may be necessary to begin with a warming-up exercise, asking the class as a whole to suggest familiar (well-worn) similes, e.g. 'as good as gold', 'as quick as a flash', and pointing out that the purpose of the exercise is not to reproduce old similes, but to create *new* ones. The first stage of the exercise will enable the students to see how this is done. During this stage, it will almost certainly emerge spontaneously that similes can also work in reverse, i.e. mean the *opposite* of what they say. For instance: 'as comfortable as an earthworm on an ice-rink', 'as warm as a moneylender's handshake'. If, however, this does not emerge, it should be brought to their attention with a few examples.

In the third stage, each group will meet *one* other group whose mime it does not need to guess (as it will be watching its own suggestions performed). This, however, is no reason for not going through with the mime, as the performing group will still need to work out the full content of the simile.

As in many other exercises, the language used in planning – and particularly in discussion – is extremely important. Here in particular one may expect vociferous disagreement: 'that doesn't work! that doesn't make sense! I don't see the point! wouldn't "silent" be better than "quiet"? how can a caterpillar have rheumatism?!' etc.

See also 3.5 Split headlines, 3.6 Split exchanges, 4.2 Emblems, 5.6 Does the humming-bird fly backwards?, 5.7 Odd news.

A SPECIMEN LIST OF SIMILES

as boring as	a dripping tap
as passionate	as a sloth on honeymoon
as clean	as a burgled safe
as red as	an overdrawn bank-account
as useful as	a bicycle on Gibraltar
as silent as	a pub at tea-time
as fresh as	a British Rail sandwich
as quick as	a Balkan waiter

FURTHER SUGGESTIONS (NO CONNECTION BETWEEN COLUMNS)

Adjectives	*Useful phrases*
calm	an elephant with toothache
serious	an eskimo in a wigwam
reliable	a politician's memoirs
graceful	champagne-and-coke
straight	a hedgehog with fleas
sincere	an oyster yawning
grey	a bath-tub with no plug
predictable	a nudist beach on Baffin island
prim	three men on a tandem
inquisitive	fishing in the Sahara
generous	Descartes in Disneyland

5.14 Words for music

What to do

A piece of impressionistic or highly striking music is played (e.g. Moussorgsky's 'Pictures at an exhibition', Mendelssohn's 'Fingal's cave overture', Aaron Copland's 'Appalachian spring' and 'Billy the kid' – it is best to choose music that is not *too* familiar). The students are told to write down one word, or several, suggested to them by the music.

They then form groups of six. The words written by each member of the group are collected. The group then tries to produce a poem using these words, and with reference to the feelings the music produced. When the poem is finished, the group presents it to another group.

A somewhat more difficult extension of this exercise is to play Mozart's 'Musical joke' (K522), a piece of music which amusingly suggests the struggles of a bad symphony writer to find a way of 'getting out' of the tangle of melodies and rhythms he has created and of finding a suitable ending. The groups are asked to listen to the music and at the same time imagine someone giving a speech and getting tangled up in his or her own words. Working alone or in pairs, they should then produce a fragment of this speech (e.g. 'The question I ask is, would it not have been easier, were we not ourselves committed to this policy, not to have agreed to refuse to be told what to do and what not to do...?'), which they 'declaim' to the others. (This is clearly for more advanced groups.)

Remarks

Level: intermediate to advanced.

This is a useful warming-up exercise for some of the work in section 7, e.g. 7.3 Colourful ideas, 7.5 Alphabet poems.

See also 4.20 Music pictures, 5.10 Random dictionary, 7.2 The time has come.

5.15 Group poem

What to do

Students work in groups of six. Each group is given one word (e.g. *snow, red, cats, pain,* etc.). Then each person in the group – without consulting anyone else – writes one sentence which the word suggests to him or her. The sentences may or may not contain the word.

The slips of paper for each group are then collected and exchanged with another group (i.e. group A gets group D's sentences, group D gets group C's, group C gets group B's, group B gets group A's).

Each group now has six sentences to work on, all relating to a single theme. The task of each group is to arrange these sentences in the best possible order to form a poem. They are allowed to discard one sentence if they wish, and/or to write one new sentence. Minor changes to grammar are also allowed to help cohesion of the fragments. Groups then present their poems to other groups.

Remarks

Level: intermediate to advanced.

A very good exercise to aid understanding of the importance of cohesion and coherence in texts.

See also 3.8 Jumbled stories, 5.3 Word for word, 5.7 Odd news, 5.13 As mixed as a metaphor, 7.3 Colourful ideas.

5.16 Word exchange

What to do

Before the session, the organizer should use a random procedure to select words for use. Ten different words for each group will be needed. (Random procedures are many and various, but simply opening the dictionary anywhere and selecting the tenth word on the left-hand page is as good as any. If the tenth word is a function word, the next content word on the page should be taken. The words should each be written on individual slips of paper.)

When the session starts, students are divided into groups of five. Each group is given ten slips. Each group must try to compose a poem of ten lines, each line containing one of the ten words.

Groups may exchange up to four words with other groups by bargaining. This must be done according to strict rules. Any group wishing to strike a bargain may send only one person to another group at any one time. And no group may receive more than one bargainer from another group at any one time.

The activity should be done within a set time limit (of e.g. fifteen minutes), after which the poems should be ready.

Remarks

Level: intermediate upwards.

The purpose of the exercise is *not* to give practice in poetry composition! Just as the purpose of exercises such as 1.50 Self-portraits was not to exercise drawing skills. Although the end product may be a poem, the language used to create this poem will be spoken prose. It may be necessary to remind students of this.

See also 5.8 News poems, 6.8 Shapes and figures, 7.6 What's in a name?

5.17 Cadavre exquis

What to do

a) At the top of a sheet of paper, each student writes a question beginning 'Why is...?', 'Why does...?', or 'What is...?' He or she then folds the paper, so as to conceal the question, and writes out the opening of the reply ('Because...' or 'It's...') before passing the sheet on to a neighbour. The neighbour writes whatever reply occurs to him or her, then passes on the sheet with a fresh question, which, as before, is concealed by folding the paper. Once the sheets have circulated several times, the results are read out aloud. These may be plausible, e.g. 'Why does alcohol have a lower freezing point than water? – Because everything is relative', or fantastic, e.g. 'Why is Mexico City a hard place to run the marathon? – Because red is the colour of danger.'

b) The same activity can then be done using a comparison instead of the question/answer. This time, the students write down the first half of a comparison: 'Travelling in a balloon is like...', or 'The smell of frying onions is like...' The paper is folded, and the word *like* written down for the comparison to be completed. Again, the results are read aloud (e.g. 'The smell of frying onions is like Bach on a rainy Sunday', etc.).

c) A variant is possible using a poem as the basis, e.g. a text such as:

If I could tell you

Time will say nothing but I told you so,
Time only knows the price we have to pay;
If I could tell you, I would let you know.

If we should weep when clowns put on their show,
If we should stumble when musicians play,
Time will say nothing but I told you so.

There are no fortunes to be told, although,
Because I love you more than I can say,
If I could tell you I would let you know.

The winds must come from somewhere when they blow,
There must be reasons why the leaves decay;
Time will say nothing but I told you so.

Perhaps the roses really want to grow,
The vision seriously intends to stay;
If I could tell you I would let you know.

Suppose the lions all get up and go,
And all the brooks and soldiers run away;
Will Time say nothing but I told you so?
If I could tell you I would let you know.

(W.H. Auden)

The students work in pairs: each pair is given only the first or only the second half of the lines, i.e. 'Time will say nothing...', 'Time only knows...', 'If I could tell you...' etc. Working together, each pair completes the lines in whatever way it likes. When this has been done, the pairs circulate, trying to find which other pair has their 'missing half'. They then compare the original text with their variants of it.

Remarks

Level: elementary to intermediate upwards.

As in many of the exercises, the purpose here is to set the mind working and stimulate the imagination by freeing words from context. The value of the activity lies not so much in what is produced as in the discussion over what 'works' or 'sounds right' and what is 'meaningless' or of no interest. Here the students will be deciding not only what is grammatically possible, but also what is satisfying to the ear and stimulating to the fancy.

Using poems, it is, of course, possible to reduce still further the initial elements, e.g. by giving only conjunctions such as *if, but, then,* or only nouns, etc.

See also 3.6 Split exchanges, 3.11 Dialogue interpretation, 4.12 Strange news, 5.7 Odd news, 5.12 Love heals all wounds, 5.13 As mixed as a metaphor.

6 Problem-solving

6.1 Castles in the air

What to do

The students work in groups of five. Each group is given two sheets of foolscap or A4-size writing paper, twelve stiff filing-cards, and thirty paper clips.

The task is as follows. Each group is to build a structure, using *all* these materials and nothing else. At the end, the criteria for success will be: *stability* (i.e. the structure should not blow over too easily!); *height* (the higher the better); *aesthetic appeal* (the more attractive it looks the better).

The activity is strictly timed (ten minutes).

After completing its structure, each group sends a judge to the next group. The group has to defend its structure to the judge, who should find counter-arguments.

Remarks

Level: elementary to intermediate upwards.

The organizer should be on hand to answer procedural questions (e.g. 'Can we tear the paper, bend the clips?' etc.), but no advice should be offered. The tightly structured and limited nature of the activity, plus the absolute time restriction, gives rise to highly functional language. With more sophisticated or advanced groups it is worth holding a feedback session in which groups discuss the roles played by each member (who was the organizer? who the technician? who the provider of ideas? etc.).

This idea was demonstrated by Jack Lonergan at a SASSET Conference in Brighton in 1978.

See also 2.7 My potato, 4.4 Potato figures.

6.2 Boxed-in

What to do

Material needed: sheets of simple non-figurative shapes, such as those below, p.189.

a) The class is divided into groups of four. In each group, one person is given half of the sheet (i.e. six figures). The others in the group, by questioning, must attempt to reconstruct these shapes as accurately as possible. While questioning, they may make trial drawings. The person with the master-sheet may not comment directly on their drawings, but may answer questions relating to them, e.g. 'Does the line look like this?...'

b) Once the six figures have been reconstructed, the drawings should be compared with the originals.

   Now, in the same groups, the students perform the reverse exercise. This time, one person is given the other half of the sheet. He or she must describe the drawings to the others, and they must attempt to reproduce them by following his or her instructions. (This may also be done in pairs, by splitting the groups of four.)

c) (Optional) In pairs, students now select one figure out of the six. They then develop a series of nine or twelve figures from this one. There should be a mathematical or logical relation between the figures. When ready, they show three of their figures to another pair. This pair then attempts to reconstruct the series by questioning.

d) The students are each given the full sheet of twelve figures. They choose one which they will alter in any way they like. They then look for anyone else who has altered the same figure. The adapted figures are compared.

e) Working in groups of three, the students prepare an exhibition. For this they will need large sheets of paper in order to 'blow up' three of the figures they have adapted. In reproducing these figures they can make further adaptations. The purpose is to produce pictures that might be exhibited, e.g. at a modern art exhibition, at a display of technical drawings, at a poster exhibition, etc. When they are ready, one person remains with the pictures, the others circulate to see the remaining exhibitions. They should enter into conversation with the person responsible for the display, criticizing, offering comments, asking for explanations, etc.

f) The groups devise their own personality test, based on interpretation of these figures after they have been transformed by the person undergoing the test. Thus, for instance, group A would take the top set of squares, group B the second, group C the third, and so on. The person taking the test will be asked to transform each square in any way he or she likes, e.g. by extending the figure beyond the limits of the square, by duplicating the shape, adding to it or creating a pattern. Each group must first draw up its own set of 'interpretations', e.g. if the figure is extended beyond the square, this is a sign of self-confidence; if a regular pattern is produced, this is a sign of insecurity; if the figure is adapted, this indicates liveliness of imagination, and so on.

The groups now split up, and each member goes to work with someone from another group. In turn, they 'test each other'. The tester offers his or her interpretation only after all the drawings have been transformed.

Finally, the groups re-form in order to compare results (and interpretations).

g) Using the same figures – without any alterations – the students work in pairs to devise plausible ways of explaining how each figure might be a *traffic-sign*. The wavy line, for instance, might indicate *corrugations* on dirt roads in east Africa; the triangle with the small circle might represent danger from large snowballs in the Alps! The suggestions may be fanciful, but they should be directly related to the figures. At the end, a round-up session could be held, with each pair offering one or two of its more enlightened ideas.

Remarks

Level: intermediate to advanced.

The material needed for this exercise is extremely simple and easy to devise. Before beginning, the students may need to be reminded of certain of the basic words – *circle, triangle, bisect, touch, parallel,* etc. – which will recur at all stages. Clearly, not all stages of the activity should be attempted in the same session.

In addition to providing valuable practice in precision of language, this activity also encourages careful listening.

See also 1.43 Backs, 2.17 Kim's game, 3.14 Inkblots, 4.3 Signs of the future, 4.20 Music pictures, 6.8 Shapes and figures.

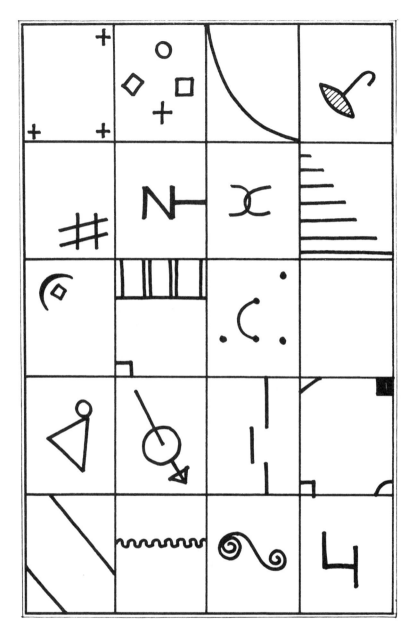

Examples of non-figurative shapes

6.3 Our choice

What to do

The students work in groups of five. Each group is a committee which administers a scholarship fund for overseas students coming to study in their country. There should, however, be *six* people on the committee. Each group therefore has to decide which of the following six people they would invite to join their committee. They are looking for someone who should not be biassed in his or her opinions and who would have plenty of time to devote to this committee.

a) *Mr Brendan Watkyn-Smythe*: sixty-five years old, with an invalid wife. He had thirty years experience as a colonial administrator, and has worked on many educational committees. Last year, he had a heart attack, but has fully recovered, and was recently elected to his local council.

b) *Celia Greenhill*: thirty years old. Single. Has had a brilliant and rapid career in a variety of jobs – advertising, administration of a college of higher education, editor of an educational magazine, etc. Was involved in a divorce scandal last year, and is said to be very ambitious. However, she has very good connections with people in power and with access to funds.

c) *Brian Groom*: forty years old. Married to a Ghanaian, with five children. All his experience has been with a local education authority. The last five years have been spent dealing with the foreign students section. He has a reputation for being efficient but lacking in human warmth.

d) *Gillian Tender*: forty years old and married to a foreign diplomat, with two children at university. Has had long experience in teaching in foreign universities, mainly in Europe, though she has travelled extensively elsewhere. She had a nervous breakdown a year ago, but has since started work as a freelance writer of children's books, and has already had one book published.

e) *Amiri Kofi:* forty-eight years old. A well-known African writer, living in exile in London. She was imprisoned for five years in Africa for her support to the opposition party. Her three children go to school in England. In spite of her experience, she is very pro-African. Last year, she remarried for the third time. Her husband is the well-known Marxist philosopher, Karl Planck.

f) *Godfrey Crane:* fifty years old. Married, with two children, both in business. Conservative MP for a wealthy area. He has travelled widely in Africa, Asia and South America, and is the Government spokesman on Commonwealth affairs. He is said to drink too much. Last year, he was invoked in a bribery case, but was cleared. A very influential person.

After making their choices, the groups should talk to each other, exchanging reasons for the choice they made.

Remarks

Level: advanced.

In many of the drama exercises – particularly those involving group productions, be it of sketches, machines, or poems – the students need to know how to listen constructively, how to put forward ideas, and, most important of all, how to *concede* a position. These are the skills which are being tested and practised in this exercise.

See also: 3.11 Dialogue interpretation, 4.10 Rules of the game, 4.18 Act Three, 7.10 Spring fever.

6.4 Faces and places

What to do

Material needed: a number of full-face portraits, and some pictures showing problem situations (for ideas see Maley, Duff and Grellet: *The Mind's Eye*).

The class is divided into groups of six. Each group is given a portrait, which it discusses in detail to extract the maximum of information. The groups then pass on their portraits, and again discuss the new portrait they receive.

The portraits are now collected, and pictures with problem situations distributed to the groups. Each group discusses its picture in order to arrive at a satisfactory interpretation of it. When all the groups are ready, they are asked to incorporate the two characters they described earlier into the situation they have just interpreted. The resulting sketch is then acted out for another group, which offers comment and criticism.

Remarks

Level: intermediate upwards.

Like the extended version of 2.17 Kim's game (3.25 Detective work), this activity allows the students to use their imagination freely while working from the same basic known elements. This means that controversy and discussion will be based on tangible 'evidence' and they will be able to refer directly to the pictures to substantiate what they have to say. The activity also, incidentally, involves considerable repetition of vocabulary and structures, since each person will be offering a different interpretation of the same actions.

See also 3.9 Telephone conversations, 3.11 Dialogue interpretation, 4.13 Starting from scratch, 7.2 The time has come.

6.5 Split cartoons

What to do

A sequential series of cartoons – see below for an example – will be needed. The class is divided into groups, so that each group has one cartoon-frame from the series. No group should show its cartoon to another.

To begin with, each group examines its cartoon very carefully, and makes detailed notes on what it contains.

Next follows the phase of information exchange. Any group may send out one person at a time to any other group to find out about its picture. Any group may also receive one visitor at a time. Each group thus tries to build up a detailed idea of each of the pictures contained in the series.

When this is done, the groups try to work out what the story of the whole sequence is. Each group then works out a dramatization of the incident, as they have interpreted it. Only after this has been done should the complete sequence be pieced together.

Remarks

Level: intermediate upwards.

Great precision – but not necessarily complexity – of language is required here. The task might well be compared to listening to instructions in a foreign language on the telephone: the more accurate the information given, the more likely it is to be correctly understood!

See also 3.6 Split exchanges, 3.21 Bringing a picture to life, 6.2 Boxed-in, 6.8 Shapes and figures.

6.6   **The secret forest**

What to do

The class is divided into pairs. One partner listens, the other talks. The listener gives the following instructions before the other begins to talk: 'I want you to imagine you are entering a forest, describe it to me.' The partner should say whatever comes into his or her mind about an imaginary forest. The listener may prompt him or her by asking: 'Tell me about the trees...' and 'Do you follow a path or do you strike off in an unknown direction?' As the storyteller continues through the forest, the listener breaks in at intervals with the following remarks:

– You see a pencil on the ground. Describe it. What do you do with it?
– You find a glass. What is it like? What do you do with it?
– You meet a bear. Describe the bear. What happens?
– You come to a river. What do you do?
– You come to a wall. Describe it.
– You come to a house. What do you do?

Once this last question has been answered, the listener will interpret the story. Only he or she knows the symbolic meaning of the objects mentioned in the questions (it will be necessary to give each listener a slip of paper with this information: pencil = creativity, glass = practicality, bear = authority, river = sex life, wall = ambition, house = death). The listener must now interpret the storyteller's attitude to life through his or her reaction to these objects.

Remarks

Level: intermediate upwards.

This exercise demands great attention on the part of the listener and some ingenuity on the part of the storyteller. It should not be tried with people who do not know each other, as the interpretation might easily be 'misinterpreted'! The symbols for the objects can of course be changed.

The idea for this exercise was suggested by Vivienne Vermes.

See also 1.44 What's in a hand?, 1.50 Self-portraits, 3.13 Palmistry, the zodiac, etc.

6.7 Alibi

What to do

The students are told that a crime has been committed and that they are under suspicion.

The class is divided into pairs. Each pair is asked to prepare an alibi for a given period of time (such as, between eight o'clock and midnight on the previous day). Since each pair claims to have spent the period in question together, both partners must be able to account for everything they might have seen, said or done.

Fifteen minutes are allowed for preparation. One pair is then chosen for interrogation. One of the partners is placed in the witness box, the other is sent out of the room. A court scene is then set up, with one student acting as the interrogator, supported by a panel of 'judges'. The 'accused' is asked to give an account of his or her activities for the period in question. While this is being done, everyone present should take careful notes. When the 'accused' has finished, additional questions may be put to him or her and the answers noted.

The second member of the pair is then called in and the same procedure followed. Clearly, the object of the game is to trick the members of a pair into making statements which do not agree.

Remarks

Level: intermediate to advanced.

This is an excellent multi-skill activity. It requires discussion within each pair, the formulation of oral questions, the retention of facts in the memory or through notes, etc.

Some help may need to be given at first with the additional questions, so that the students understand how to catch out the 'accused'. For example, 'What was the weather like when you came home?' If this has not been thought of by the pair, the first student will have to say something, and this may not be corroborated by his or her accomplice. Once such 'tricks' have been discovered, however, the activity takes off on its own, and the questions come thick and fast.

With larger classes, the students can be divided into groups of four instead of pairs. Only one member of the group goes outside, the remaining three being questioned together.

See also 1.56 and 1.57 Childhood memories (1 and 2), 1.63 Identikit, 2.8 Familiar scenes, 2.12 Clues, 2.15 I say, you said, he said, 6.3 Our choice.

6.8   Shapes and figures

What to do

Material needed: for variant 1, sets of shapes (see below); for variant 2, several large sheets of stiff, coloured paper.

Variant 1
The class is divided into groups of two or three. Each group is given a set of shapes. (These could be reproduced by members of the class during their spare time.) Each group now constructs a figure using all the elements (as in the figure below). When the figure is ready, they should make a quick sketch of it and then write down clearly and concisely the instructions for making this figure, e.g.

1   Place the largest triangle *over* the bottom left-hand corner of the square. The corner point of the square should meet the middle of the longest side of the triangle.
2   Place the thinnest triangle upside down, so that its top point meets the middle of the top side of the square.
3   Place the remaining triangle against the bottom right hand corner of the square, so that the shortest side of the triangle continues the bottom side of the square.

Once it has written out these instructions, each group breaks up its figure and exchanges instructions with another group. Each group now tries to reconstitute another group's figure, following the written instructions it has been given. When ready, the groups inspect each other's work, comment and criticize. There will of course be two kinds of criticism: group A (observing) – 'You didn't follow the instructions properly!', group B (reconstructing) – 'Your instructions weren't clearly written!' This discussion should be encouraged to develop, with each group offering suggestions as to how the instructions might be improved.

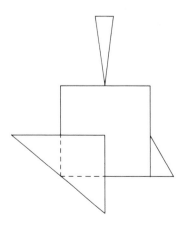

Variant 2

Bartering: This is an entertaining variant of the preceding exercise, involving language of quite a different order.

Six large sheets of stiff, coloured paper – all of different colours – are cut into identical shapes (see diagram below). The class is divided into six groups (it does not matter if the groups are of different sizes). The pieces of coloured paper are now shuffled and distributed at random to the six groups. Thus, one group may have three orange pieces, two green, four red and no blue, while another might have three blue, one red, two orange and no green. One group may also have more or fewer pieces than another. The purpose is for each group to reconstruct a complete sheet of one colour. To do this, they may send two emissaries round to barter with other groups, offering pieces of one colour in exchange for those of another.

It will inevitably happen that two groups will begin collecting pieces of the same colour. Clearly, one of them will have to switch at some stage to a different colour. Which group this is will depend on which is best at bartering! No group may deliberately withhold a piece merely to slow down the work of another group, but they may impose certain conditions, e.g. 'We'll give you the red piece in exchange for two blues', or 'We'll give you the piece you want if you can describe its shape!'

At this stage, i.e. when most of the groups have settled on one colour, it may be necessary for the class to be reminded that the task is not finished until the jig-saw has been completed. This means that the groups which were slow in bartering may still have a chance to catch up.

The first group to complete its sheet is the 'winner'.

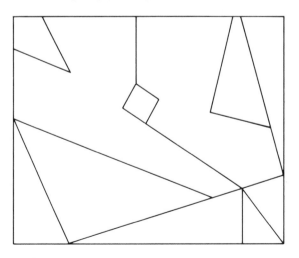

Each coloured sheet is cut into small pieces of exactly the same shape

Remarks

Level: intermediate upwards.

Although the first exercise is not in itself a drama activity, it provides excellent practice in two kinds of language – giving/receiving instructions and comment/criticism – both of which are indispensable for drama work.

In variant 2 (Bartering), the emphasis is, of course, on the language of interaction – persuasion, offering and rejecting, agreement and disagreement, etc. Here the problem cannot be solved merely by following instructions.

What we have outlined here are two models, on which innumerable variants are possible, e.g. a written element could be introduced by having fragments of sentences written on the pieces of paper; or the shapes could be introduced as an extra element in other exercises involving construction, design or information transfer.

See also 1.8 Remaking the web, 2.2 Freeze!, 3.22 Picture sets, 4.4 Potato figures, 4.5 Cork, stone and wood, 4.10 Rules of the game, 6.1 Castles in the air, 6.2 Boxed in, 6.5 Split cartoons.

6.9 Maps

What to do

Material needed: one large wall-map of the world (or several smaller maps).

As a warming-up exercise, the students are asked to write down the names of five large cities, two rivers and two mountain ranges. Next to each, they note as precisely as possible the positions of the cities, rivers and mountain ranges (longitude, latitude, proximity of other cities etc.). If the class is not too large, each student is asked to call out one name from his or her list with location details. A well-known capital city such as London should be sited not only in terms of English geography but also *comparatively*, e.g. 'If you move in a straight line east of London, the only major European city close to this line is Leipzig; or Madrid and New York lie almost on the same latitude.'

With larger classes, the students should form groups of four and perform the same exercise.

The class is now divided into pairs. Partner A is given three to five minutes to study the map; partner B uses this time to compile as many questions as possible on world geography. The kind of questions that partner B might ask are, for instance:
– What countries border on Czechoslovakia?

– Which city is further from Warsaw, Helsinki or Moscow?
– What countries does the river Nile run through?
– If you follow a straight line east or west from the southernmost tip
   of New Zealand, what land do you strike?
– Which is larger, Ireland or Albania?

The pairs now join up again: partner B asks the questions, and partner A answers as accurately as possible. Before checking the answers
against the map, each pair must join with another pair to compare
questions and answers. Both pairs comment on the accuracy of each
other's work. The map is then consulted as the final 'arbiter'.

Remarks

Level: elementary to intermediate upwards.

   This exercise may be taken as a model for the kind of problem-
solving activity that can be based on knowledge of other subjects
(e.g. history, physics, mathematics).

   As it stands, it is purely a problem-solving activity. It is, however,
not difficult to make a bridge with drama. For instance, working in
groups of four (i.e. two of the original pairs), the students create a
mime sequence involving two of the cities, one river and one mountain range, e.g. Stockholm, Vladivostok, the Danube, and the
Himalayas. The observing group must then identify the respective
elements.

See also 3.7 Mixed sets, 3.18 The hotel receptionist, 5.3 Word for
word, 7.6 What's in a name?

7 The use of literary texts, poems and songs

7.1 As you like it

What to do

Members of the class are told to find those whose likes and dislikes in music are closest to their own. Each person should try to talk to everyone in the class before selecting partners. Small groups – varying from two to six members – will now be formed from people with similar interests.

A well-known, popular melody is proposed, e.g. 'Yellow submarine', 'Singin' in the rain', 'Yesterday' etc. This should preferably be a song with a melody and words that are easy to remember. The song should then be sung several times by the whole group. (If necessary, a record can be played.)

Each group is asked to adapt the song to suit the kind of music they prefer. Thus, for instance, the 'folk' group will transform it into a folk song; the 'baroque' group into, perhaps, a baroque concerto; the 'opera' group into an opera, etc. It is up to each group to decide how much they wish to adapt the words or melody. Considerable freedom may be allowed.

When they have 'rehearsed', the groups perform for each other.

Remarks

Level: elementary upwards.

This exercise is likely to work best with adults, as the range of their musical interests will be wide enough to allow different groups to form. Although the end product is a piece of music, it should not be forgotten that much language – particularly the language of suggestion – will be needed in the preparation. Apart from being enjoyable in itself, the exercise is useful for 'getting things going' at the beginning of a session.

See also 1.28 Slow motion, 1.38 Becoming a musical instrument, 4.20 Music pictures, 5.14 Words for music.

7.2   The time has come

What to do

Material needed: a number of short, preferably non-explicit texts. (Several ideas are given below. Since suitable texts are difficult to find in books, it is best to produce one's own.)

The class is divided into four or six groups (three people to a group). Then the texts are distributed: the same text should be given to two groups. Each group reads its text silently before discussing it. The purpose of the exercise is to transform the text by giving it a specific meaning. In order to reveal this meaning more clearly, the groups are asked to work out the language – written or spoken – that precedes and follows the text. In short, they have to provide the surrounding context. No words may be changed in the text itself, but complete freedom of interpretation is allowed. When ready, each group presents its text to the rest of the class: one person reads or speaks the introduction, one reads the original text, and one the conclusion. (It is suggested that *before* the presentation is made, the text be read once in a neutral voice, with no inflexion or emphasis.)

Remarks

Level: intermediate upwards.

Many skills are being practised here. One of the most important of these is the ability to give meaning to language through changes of intonation.

It should be pointed out that a further great value of the exercise is that it offers an outlet for imaginative work based on controlled language.

See also 3.6 Split exchanges, 3.18 The hotel receptionist, 7.3 Colourful ideas, 7.4 Starters.

IDEAS FOR TEXTS

1   The time is not right, you say. But is it ever right? It is not the time that must be right for us, but we who must be right for the time. What does this mean? It means that we must be ready at every moment. Ready to act or not to act. To go or not to go. To stay or not to stay. Think of the proverb 'Look before you leap'. Then think of the proverb 'He who hesitates is lost'. Is this a time to hesitate or a time to leap? Only *you* can say. And the time has come to speak.

2   Take the example of the weaver bird. With great care, he builds a nest. When he thinks it is ready, and only then, he shows it to his mate. She inspects it, carefully. And if she finds a fault, she flies away. And the weaver bird begins to build a new nest. He may have to build fifty nests

before his mate is satisfied. Each one is a labour of love. Is there not a lesson to be learnt from this remarkable bird?

3 It was an idea known to the ancient Egyptians. And to the Greeks and the Romans. We find it – in a different form of course – in the Renaissance. And again in the Middle Ages. Industrialization could not kill it. It is something that has survived. That must survive. That will survive. Yet now, in the twentieth century, it would seem to be dying. Or dead. Why? we ask.

4 Figures are not all. What does a hundred mean, or a thousand? Nor is size as important as we think. What is big? What is small? All is relative. What is important, then? Time? Space? Freedom of movement? Perhaps. But surely, what matters most is knowing that the fire is still burning and that the lights have not gone out.

5 Black. Green. Yellow. Red. These are not just colours. They are more than colours. Each has a quality of its own. A different quality. How can we discover this if we do not search? But you can search and find, and you can search and not find. There are those for whom green and red, yellow and black are still no more than colours. They are the ones who have searched but have not found.

7.3 Colourful ideas

What to do

The material needed is set out below. Not all the texts need be used: a selection of four or five would be sufficient.

For the first stage, the class is divided into pairs. Each pair is given copies of the texts and asked to read and discuss them. In the discussion, they should concentrate particularly on the function of *colour* in each text, and on questions such as: 'Who is the text written by?' 'For what kind of reader?' 'For what purpose?' etc. The discussion is informal: once the students have exchanged ideas with their partners, they should be encouraged to circulate and talk to others. Approximately fifteen minutes are allowed for the first stage.

In the second stage, they should work in groups of three. Their task is to compose a *new* passage, made up entirely of fragments of the original passages. These may be combined in any way and in any order, provided the original wording is not changed. No words may be added. The new passage should not be longer than six sentences. Each member of the group then *memorizes* two sentences, so that the passage can be spoken aloud – not read – with alternating voices. Once a group is ready, it finds another group with which to exchange passages.

Remarks

Level: intermediate to advanced.

As in many exercises in this book, the purpose here is to give words fresh meaning by taking them out of context. The memorization is important because it helps to make the interpretation personal.

This is, of course, only one way in which these texts might be used. Another exercise, particularly suitable at advanced level, is to get the students to read the texts and then, working in pairs, produce passages in which the colour yellow is explored from different points of view, e.g.

– as a symbol (e.g. in anthropology or semiology)
– as stimulus to a recollection (e.g. in a play or film script)
– as a colour in itself (e.g. a fashion house or car manufacturer deciding to launch yellow as the 'colour of the season')
– as an association (e.g. in a child's mind, linked to the colour of his Latin text-book)

In order to take this exercise beyond the mechanical stage of writing, the students should be asked to prepare a monologue or dialogue, which could then be spoken to others.

See also 3.9 Telephone conversations, 3.11 Dialogue interpretation, 5.7 Odd news, 5.10 Random dictionary, 5.13 As mixed as a metaphor.

TEXTS

1 And there they were, the yellow daffodils, and nobody seemed to care. They were there for decorative purposes that had no meaning at all; and as you watched them their yellow brilliance filled the noisy room. Colour has this strange effect on the eye. It wasn't so much that the eye absorbed the colour, as that the colour seemed to fill your being. You *were* that colour; you didn't become that colour – you were of it.
(*The second Penguin Krishnamurti reader*)

2 Yellow is obtained by combining red with green light. Young suggested that yellow is always seen by effective red-green mixture, there being no separate type of receptor sensitive to yellow light, but rather two sets of receptors sensitive respectively to red and green, the combined activity of which gives the sensation yellow. Perhaps the fulcrum of controversies over colour theories is the perception of yellow. Is yellow seen by combined activity of red + green systems, or is it *primary*?
(R. Gregory, *The eye and the brain*)

3 Deeper still. The peritoneum, pink and gleaming and membranous, bulges into the wound. It is grasped with the forceps and opened... The sense of trespassing is keener now, heightened by the world's light illuminating the organs, their secret colours revealed – maroon and salmon and yellow. The vista is sweetly vulnerable at this moment, a kind of welcoming. An arc of the liver shines high and on the right, like a dark

sun. It laps over the pink sweep of the stomach, from whose lower border
the gauzy omentum is draped, and through which veil one sees, sinuous,
slow as just-fed snakes, the indolent coils of the intestine.
(Richard Selzer, *Mortal licence*)

4   I am hard at it, painting with the enthusiasm of a Marseillais eating bouil-
labaisse, which won't surprise you when you know what I'm at is the
painting of some great sunflowers. I have three canvases in hand – 1st,
three huge flowers in a green vase; 2nd, three flowers, one gone to seed,
stripped of its petals; and another in bud against a royal blue
background; 3rd, twelve flowers and buds in a yellow vase...So the whole
thing will be a symphony in blue and yellow.
(Vincent van Gogh, Letters)

5   This means that any simple account of colour vision is doomed to failure:
colour depends not only on the stimulus wavelengths and intensities, but
also on differences of intensity between regions, and whether the patterns
are accepted as representing objects...The eye tends to accept as white not
a particular mixture of colours but rather the general illumination. Thus
we see a car's headlamps as white while on a country drive, but in town
where there are bright lights for comparison, they look quite yellow.
(R. Gregory, *The eye and the brain*)

6   Poem instead of a photograph
                      (for John and Ann)

               green   grass
            dappled with darkgreen shadow
      empty winebottles tablecloth pale orange melon rinds
      Ann pink towelling dress against darkgreen bushes
            holding Esther in pale violet dress
             one pink flower in the background
            (Adrian Henri)

7   Many philosophers say that it is logically possible for men to be immediately acquainted with God, as they are immediately acquainted with
a sense content, and that there is no reason why one should be prepared to
believe a man when he says that he is seeing a yellow patch, and refuse to
believe him when he says that he is seeing God... But, ordinarily, the man
who says that he is seeing God is saying not merely that he is experiencing
a religious emotion, but also that there exists a transcendent being who is
the object of this emotion; just as the man who says that he sees a yellow
patch is ordinarily saying not merely that his visual sense-field contains a
yellow sense content, but also that there exists a yellow object to which
the sense content belongs.
(A.J. Ayer, *Language, truth and logic*)

8   Now, in the Castilian scene, distance was hard and taciturn. The colours
themselves were harsher in the foreground and there was, above all, an
exact sight of shape and line...Rock was rock, trees were trees, mountains
were mountains, and wilderness was wilderness. I was being cured. It is
true that the clarity of the Castilian air was a novelty to a northerner in
whose country mistiness and uncertainty blur the edges of objects and
feelings. Here one began to see exactly...One of the curious sights of the

journey, when darkness came, was the blackness of the dark, the nearness and size of the stars, and the yellow lights, scattered and individual, of distant towns.
(V.S. Pritchett, *Midnight oil*)

7.4 **Starters** (Short stories)

What to do

Material needed: photocopies of the openings of a few short stories. Suggestions are given below.

The class is divided into groups of four or five. Each group is given the opening of a story (they need not all work from different stories; if there are, for instance, six groups, three different openings could be used).

Using the opening as a starting-point, the groups work out a dramatized short story, which may be either mimed or spoken. Twenty minutes are given for preparation; each group then presents its story to the others. *Note*: at some stage, not necessarily the beginning, the opening should be read to the observers.

Remarks

Level: advanced.

If possible, the full text of the story should be made available for students who wish to compare their version with the original.

This exercise is the last – and possibly the most complex – in a series of similar exercises running throughout the book.

See also 3.21 Bringing a picture to life, 3.22 Picture sets, 3.26 The envelope, 4.5 Cork, stone and wood, 4.18 Act Three, 4.19 Waking dream, 5.7 Odd news, 7.2 The time has come, 7.3 Colourful ideas.

OPENINGS OF SHORT STORIES

1 One dollar and eighty-seven cents. That was all. And sixty cents of it was in pennies. Pennies saved one and two at a time by bulldozing the grocer and the vegetable man and the butcher until one's cheeks burned with the silent imputation of parsimony that such close dealing implied. Three times Della counted it. One dollar and eight-seven cents. And the next day would be Christmas.
   (O. Henry, 'The gift of the Magi')

2 At midnight the café was crowded. By some chance the little table at which I sat had escaped the eye of incomers, and two vacant chairs at it extended their arms with venal hospitality to the influx of patrons.
   And then a cosmopolite sat in one of them, and I was glad, for I held a

theory that since Adam no true citizen of the world has existed. We hear
of them, and we see foreign labels on much luggage, but we find travel-
lers instead of cosmopolites.
(O. Henry, 'A cosmopolite in a café')

3 Eight o'clock in the morning. Miss Ada Moss lay in a black iron
bedstead, staring up at the ceiling. Her room, a Bloomsbury top-floor
back, smelled of soot and face powder and the paper of fried potatoes
she brought in for supper the night before. 'Oh, dear', thought Miss
Moon, 'I am cold. I wonder why it is that I always wake up cold in the
mornings now...'
(Katherine Mansfield, 'Pictures')

4 These days, when people emigrate, it is not so much in search of sunshine,
or food, or even servants. It is fairly safe to say that the family bound for
Australia, or wherever it may be, has in its mind a vision of a nice house,
or a flat, with maybe a bit of garden. I don't know how things were a
hundred or fifty years ago. It seems from books, that the colonizers and
adventurers went sailing off to a new fine life, a new country...
(Doris Lessing, 'A Home for the Highland Cattle')

5 'And where's Mr Campbell?' Charlie asked.
'Gone to Switzerland. Mr Campbell's a pretty sick man, Mr Wales.'
'I'm sorry to hear that. And George Hardt?' Charlie inquired.
'Back in America, gone to work.'
'And where is the Snow Bird?'
'He was in here last week. Anyway, his friend, Mr Schaeffer is in Paris.'
Two familiar names from the long list of a year and a half ago.
Charlie scribbled an address in his notebook and tore out the page.
'If you see Mr Schaeffer, give him this. It's my brother-in-law's address. I
haven't settled on a hotel yet.'
He was not really disappointed to find Paris was so empty.
(Scott Fitzgerald, 'Babylon revisited')

6 A message came from the rescue party, who straightened up and leaned
on their spades in the rubble. The policeman said to the crowd: 'Everyone
keep quiet for five minutes. No talking, please. They're trying to hear
where he is.'
(V.S. Pritchett, 'The voice')

7.5 Alphabet poems

What to do

As a warming-up exercise, 1.6 Body numbers or 1.37 Body words
could be tried.

The students are then asked to pair off. They should discuss any
associations that letters may have for them (e.g. their own initials,
letters they have seen carved or inscribed in strange places, letters
they find difficult to write, letters that remind them of people, places,

colours, sounds, etc.). Each pair should then join with another to exchange impressions.

Five to eight minutes are allowed for these discussions, then the poems and extracts below are read out or they may be photocopied and distributed. These are intended only as a stimulus, to set the mind working. Each pair should now try to work out its own novel way of presenting the alphabet by giving it a particular slant, e.g. an alphabet for explorers/businessmen/young lovers/hypochondriacs/tourists/politicians etc. Once they are ready – it is not necessary to do *all* the letters systematically – they exchange their alphabets with others.

Remarks

Level: intermediate upwards.

Students may find it easier to concentrate their thoughts if they are told to decide from the start on a specific title, e.g. 'An alphabet for café-waiters'...'A is for aperitif, B is for beer, C is for coffee – but we don't serve it here!' etc.

See also 1.43 Backs, 4.14 Amazimbi, 5.8 News poems.

TEXTS FOR 'ALPHABET POEMS'

1 A is for atlas, but I am not in it.
B is for beehive, but I have no honey.
C is for cheesecloth, but I shall not materialize.
D is for Darwin, but I am a mutation.
E is for ecstasy, beyond your apprehension.
F is for fools – how are you, my friends?
G is for gunfire, all in the day's work etc.
(Edwin Morgan)

2 The alphabetic adverts in lonely hearts column of *Time Out*

– Zingaro, yodeller, xenophobe, wisecracker, voyager, utopianist, trentagenarian, soliloquist, romantic, quidnunc, pyrrhonist, oddball, nucivore, marionette, Londoner, kafkaphile, jaywalker, individualist, heterosexual, guruphobe, fatalist, eclectic, dreamer, caucasian, bacchanal, atheist, seeks female companionship. Box°°°
– Anachronism, bacchanal, carpet-monger, dilettante, eccentric, flibbertigibbet, galumpher, heterosexual, inaniloquist, jaywalker, knucklehead, Londoner, marionette, nyctaphile, optimist, punster, quidnunc, romantic, stargazer, Taurean, unicyclist, voyeur, weirdo, yodeller, zetetic, late thirties, seeks female companionship. Box°°°

3 Little alphabet of the monks in the school of Christ

Aspire to be unknown, and to be accounted nothing; for this is more beautiful and profitable for thee than the praise of men.

Be benevolent to all thy fellows, alike to the good and to the evil; and be burdensome to none.

Care for it that thy heart be kept from wandering thoughts, thy mouth from vain speech, thy senses under discipline.

Dwell in solitude and silence, and therein shalt thou find great peace and a good conscience; for in a multitude are much noise and many distractions of the heart.

Elect poverty and simplicity and be content with a few things, and thou wilt not be quick to complain.

Flee the conversation of worldly men...

(St Thomas à Kempis)

4 A – The Absolutely Abstemious Ass,
           who resided in a Barrel, and only lived on
           Soda Water and Pickled Cucumbers.

   B – The Bountiful Beetle,
           who always carried a Green Umbrella when it didn't rain,
           and left it at home when it did.

   C – The Comfortable Confidential Cow,
           who sate in her Red Morocco Arm Chair and
           toasted her own Bread at the parlour Fire.

   D – The Dolomphious Duck...

   (Edward Lear)

5 Alphobiabet

...

Claustrophobia, or the Nomad's Energy –
fear of coffins and the city's padded cell.

Dendrophobia, or Macbeth's Disease –
fear of lumberjacks and falling leaves.

Equaphobia, or the Centaur's Dilemma –
fear of the senses' rash stampede, the motor car's undoing.

Faecophobia, or Kilroy's Fever –
fear of nappies, of putting one's foot in it.

Gallophobia, or The Snail's Petition –
the potent man's aversion to missives from France.

...

Ideophobia, or Definition's Give-away –
fear of rhetoric and the blind man's banter.

Jargonophobia, or Sociology's Cancer –
fear of Art Historians and the Semantic's chair.

(Stewart Brown)

7.6   What's in a name?

What to do

The class is divided into groups of three or four. First, each group compiles a list of proper names, each group working on a different list. These lists could include, for instance, the names of:
– rivers throughout the world
– living political figures
– capital or major cities
– historical figures
– wild animals
– authors, musicians, painters etc.
Once the list has been established, the names must be placed in a rhythmical sequence to make a chant which can be read aloud.

Remarks

Level: elementary upwards.

This is not a difficult exercise, and it should not be made difficult by complicating the instructions. It is essential to concentrate only on the names and on their rhythmic combination. Although it can obviously serve as an entertaining way of teaching the pronunciation of the names of countries, nations, languages, etc., this purpose should not be made explicit as it may distract from the pleasure of the exercise.

Extracts from three poems, which might serve as examples, are given below.

Note: The groups could, of course, work on the same topic, or even on mixed topics.

See also 1.19 Beat out that rhythm, 3.7 Mixed sets, 6.9 Maps.

EXAMPLES

1 Me

(*If you weren't you, who would you like to be?*)

Paul McCartney   Gustav Mahler
Alfred Jarry   John Coltrane
Charlie Mingus   Claude Debussy
Wordsworth Monet   Bach and Blake

Charlie Parker   Pierre Bonnard
Leonardo   Bessie Smith
Fidel Castro   Jackson Pollock
Gaudi Milton   Munch and Berg

Béla Bartok   Henri Rousseau
Rauschenberg and Jasper Johns
Lukas Cranach   Shostakovich
Kropotkin   Ringo George and John...

Guillaume Apollinaire
Cannonball   Adderley
René Magritte
Hieronymous Bosch...
                    and last of all
                              me.

(Adrian Henri)

2   Bombay, Brussels, Riga, Rekjavik,
     Galway, Lagos, Lima, Zurich,
     Strasbourg, Luxembourg
     Montreal, Kabul,
     Baghdad, Volgograd,
     Istanbul, Hull.

     Stockholm, Athens, Cannes, Dubrovnik
     Bangkok, Ankara, Rabat, Windhoek
     Warsaw, Wellington,
     Belfast, Lisbon,
     Auckland, Samarkand, Durban, Brisbane
             Ottawa, Salermo
             Cairo, Tirana
             Canberra, Colombo
             Rio, Lhasa
             Oslo, Geneva
             Havana, Vienna
             Leningrad, Tallin
             Szeged, Madrid

     Delhi, Shanghai, Papeete, Entebbe
       Pula, Peking, Pondicherry
     Budapest, Bucharest, Belfast, Bergen
       Tunis, Algiers, Copenhagen
         Bratislava, Calcutta,
         Lisbon, Turin,
         Addis-Ababa
         Bonn, Berlin
     London, Dublin, Jo'burg, Turku
     Tripoli, Helsinki, Timbuctu.

     (Alan Duff)

3 An animal alphabet

Alligator, beetle, porcupine, whale,
Bobolink, panther, dragon-fly, snail,
Crocodile, monkey, buffalo, hare,
Dromedary, leopard, mud-turtle, bear,
Elephant, badger, pelican, ox,
Flying-fish, reindeer, anaconda, fox,
Guinea-pig, dolphin, antelope, goose,
Humming-bird, weasel, pickerel, moose.

(Anonymous)

7.7 Computer poems

What to do

The class is divided into groups of three. Each group should draw up a short list of three or four popular expressions, e.g. 'Happy birthday', 'How do you do', 'Don't mention it'. The lists are then collected and redistributed. Each group, now working from a new list, passes *one* of these messages through the 'computer' to produce a result similar to that of Edwin Morgan's 'The Computer's First Christmas Card' (text below). Each member of the group should take part in 'delivering' the computer poem aloud to other groups.

Two other poems – suggesting different ways of developing the same idea – are also given below.

Remarks

Level: elementary upwards.

This could also serve as preparation for other exercises, such as 4.16 Making a machine and 7.10 Spring fever.

Variants on the idea as outlined above would include:

– producing computer songs, using as components either the titles of familiar songs ('Singin' in the rain', 'Yesterday', etc.) or the words of popular songs;

– producing poems or songs by feeding the 'computer' with completely disparate elements, e.g. newspaper headlines, book titles, proverbs, quotations, brand names (Nescafé, Maserati, White Horse) etc.

See also 4.14 Amazimbi, 5.6 Does the humming-bird fly backwards?, 5.8 News poems, 5.13 As mixed as a metaphor.

EXAMPLES
The computer's first Christmas card

jollymerry
hollyberry
jollyberry
merryholly
happyjolly
jollyjelly
jollybelly
bellymerry
hollyheppy
jollyMolly
marryJerry
merryHarry
hoppyBarry
heppyJarry
boppyheppy
berryjorry
moppyjelly
Mollymerry
Jerryjolly
bellyboppy
jorryhoppy
hollymoppy
Barrymerry
Jarryhappy
happyboppy
boppyjolly
jollymerry
merrymerry
merrymerry
merryChris
ammerryasa
Chrismerry
asMERRYCHR
YSANTHEMUM

(Edwin Morgan)

The taxes of sin

No one knows the woman I love.
The woman knows I love no one.
I love no one the woman knows.
The woman knows no one I love.
No one knows I love the woman.
I love the woman no one knows.
No one I love knows the woman.
The woman no one knows I love.

(Alan Maley)

The first men on Mercury

- We come in peace from the third planet
  Would you take us to your leader?
- Bawr stretter! Bawr. Bawr Stretterhawl?
- This is a little plastic model
  of the solar system, with working parts.
  You are here and we are there, and we
  are now here with you, is this clear?
- Gawl horrop. Bawr! Abawrhannahanna!
- Where we come from is blue and white
  with brown, you see we call the brown
  here 'land', the blue is 'sea', we live
  on the surface of the brown land,
  all round is sea and clouds. We are 'men'.
  Men come –
- Glawp men! Gawrbenner menko. Menhawl?
- Men come in peace from the third planet
  which we call 'earth'. We are earthmen.
  Take us earthmen to your leader.
- Thmen? Thmen? Bawr. Bawrhossop.
  Yuleeda tan hanna. Harrabost yuleeda.
- I am the yuleeda. You see my hands,
  we carry no benner, we come in peace.
  The spaceways are all stretterhawn.
- Glawn peacemen all horrabhanna tantko!
  Tan come at'mstrossop. Glawp yuleeda!
- Atoms are peacegawl in our harraban.
  Menbat worrabost from tanhannahanna.
- You men we know bawrhossoptant. Bawr.
  We know yuleeda. Go strawg backspetter quick.
- We cantantabwar, tantingko backspetter now!
- Banghapper now! Yes, third planet back.
  Yuleeda will go back blue, white, brown
  nowhanna! There is no more talk.
- Gawl han fasthapper...?
- No. You must go back to your planet.
  Go back in peace, take what you have gained
  but quickly.
- Stretterworra gawl gawl...
- Of course, but nothing is ever the same,
  now is it? You'll remember Mercury.

(Edwin Morgan)

It's all in the mind

It is all in the mind
The mind is all in it.
Is it all in the mind?
All the mind is in it.
In it is all the mind.
In the mind it all is.
It is the mind in all.

(Alan Duff)

7.8   Love is...

What to do

Material needed: poems in which a strong central idea is developed
in a way that can be easily imitated. Three examples are given below.

The class is first divided into an even number of smaller groups
(four, six or eight). Two poems are then read aloud to the class as a
whole. If there are, for example, six groups, three will be asked to
work on one poem and three on the other. From the one poem, the
theme chosen will be 'Love is...', from the other 'When I am an old
woman (or man) I shall...' In each group, the members will work out
three or four lines of their own, relating to the source idea but not
necessarily to the original poem. It should be stressed that the purpose is not to produce a different version of the poem, but to develop
the central idea. The group then discusses the ideas it has produced.
Five or six of the best lines are then selected, and these are combined
to make a new poem. When complete, the poems are read aloud.

Remarks

Level: intermediate to advanced.

In spite of what one may think, no real poetic skill is required for
this exercise. (For reassurance, the group could be read some of the
poems of Ogden Nash, as examples of how flexible rhythm and line
length can be.) A feeling for the sound of the language will, however,
be brought out when the group comes to the stage of putting its poem
together. Here there may be considerable – and useful – disagreement.

See also 2.10 Listening with eyes closed, 5.8 News poems, 5.12 Love
heals all wounds, 7.3 Colourful ideas.

EXAMPLES

How do I love thee?

How do I love thee? Let me count the ways.
I love thee to the depth and breadth and height
My soul can reach, when feeling out of sight
For the ends of Being and ideal Grace.
I love thee to the level of every day's
Most quiet need, by sun and candle-light.
I love thee freely, as men strive for right;
I love thee purely, as they turn from praise.
I love thee with the passion put to use
In my old griefs, and with my childhood's faith.
I love thee with a love I seemed to lose
With my lost saints – I love thee with the breath,
Smiles, tears, of all my life! – and, if God choose,
I shall but love thee better after death.

(Elizabeth Barrett Browning, 'Sonnets from the Portuguese')

Warning

When I am an old woman I shall wear purple
With a red hat which doesn't go, and doesn't suit me,
And I shall spend my pension on brandy and summer gloves
And satin sandals, and say we've no money for butter.
I shall sit down on the pavement when I'm tired
And gobble up samples in shops and press alarm bells
And run my stick along the public railings
And make up for the sobriety of my youth.
I shall go out in my slippers in the rain
And pick flowers in other people's gardens
And learn to spit.

(Jenny Joseph)

Love is...

Love is feeling cold in the back of vans
Love is a fanclub with only two fans
Love is walking holding paintstained hands
Love is

Love is fish and chips on winter nights
Love is blankets full of strange delights
Love is when you don't put out the light
Love is

Love is presents in Christmas shops
Love is when you're feeling Top of the Pops
Love is what happens when the music stops
Love is

Love is white panties lying all forlorn
Love is a pink nightdress still slightly warm
Love is when you have to leave at dawn
Love is

Love is you and love is me
Love is a prison and love is free
Love's what's there when you're away from me
Love is

(Adrian Henri)

7.9 Amnesty

What to do

For warming-up exercises, see *Remarks* below.

The students are told to find a space for themselves, to sit down in this space and close their eyes. (If possible, nobody should be within touching distance of anyone else.) This space is a prison cell.

The way in which the exercise now develops will depend on the class's level.

1 FOR INTERMEDIATE CLASSES

The students are told that they have been in solitary confinement for one month. During this time they have not spoken to anyone. Soon, they will be taken out to the exercise yard, where they will meet the other solitary confinement prisoners. Before going out to exercise, the 'prisoners' should concentrate on any thoughts that may have obsessed them during confinement. They should think particularly of anything they cannot remember, e.g. the words of a song, the name of the President of a country, the author of a book, the title of a film etc. This recollection should be done, eyes closed, sitting or lying on the ground.

After two to four minutes, the prisoners are told to form a circle in the exercise yard. They are to walk round, slowly, in a clockwise direction with their hands behind their backs. They are not allowed to talk, but they may try to whisper to each other. (The organizer will act as 'guard'.) They should all try to find out as much as they can from their immediate neighbours.

After about two minutes, the prisoners are divided into groups of four to six, and sent to larger cells. In each cell, they discuss the questions that were running through their minds, particularly those to which nobody knows the answer. While they are discussing, the organizer informs them that they may soon be released as part of an amnesty agreement.

Now, two prisoners from each cell are moved to another cell. The newcomers exchange impressions with the other prisoners.

Finally, all the prisoners are herded together, awaiting release. Each should now try to find any others who have been worrying over the same questions. The discussion should be allowed to continue for at least five minutes.

2 FOR ADVANCED CLASSES

The procedure is as in 1, with the changes in focus indicated below:

a) *Non native-speakers:* with advanced students, the exercise can be made more demanding by restricting the questions to be discussed. The prisoners can be told, for instance, to concentrate exclusively on recalling the dates and places of events that have occurred in the past six months, i.e. prior to their imprisonment. Or, if they all share lessons in other subjects, they may be asked to recall as much as they can of e.g. a novel, a specific event in history, etc.

b) *Native-speakers:* may be asked to recall as much as they can of, for example, familiar quotations (e.g. 'I have measured out my life with coffee-spoons' – for ideas, see the *Oxford Book of Quotations*), the words of songs/poems/hymns/anthems (verse 2 of 'God save the Queen'?), names of provincial towns, politicians, sportsmen, journalists etc. In short, any aspect of the life and culture of their own country.

c) *Specialist groups:* e.g. doctors, engineers, may be asked to recall facts relating to their profession, e.g. physical/chemical laws, definitions, rules/regulations, diagnoses and clinical symptoms, the qualities of certain metals or materials etc.

Remarks

This is an extremely rich exercise, but it is also very demanding. If it is to work, it is essential that the right mood be created from the start. Several of the exercises from section 1, e.g. 1.25 Feeling my space, 1.56 and 1.57 Childhood memories (1 and 2), 1.27 From seed to plant, will help to create an atmosphere of relaxed concentration. One of the two passages below might also be read aloud.

The experience of solitary confinement should not become traumatic, and so it is up to the organizer to introduce the idea of a possible *amnesty* early on in the exercise. It must be remembered that the focus of the exercise is on *human contact* after isolation. The pacing, then, should be unhurried, with the students being given time to come up with questions to which they genuinely want to know the answers. The last stage of the exercise should be allowed to develop into open discussion.

Although this is a relatively complex activity, it need not be linguistically demanding. Each student is free to determine his or her own questions, and even the discussion will be controlled as it will concentrate mainly on the *confirmation* or *correction* of statements. The interest is generated by the suspense of not knowing and wanting to know.

See also 1.43 Backs, 2.8 Familiar scenes, 2.14 If I remember rightly..., 2.18 Lost memory, 3.7 Mixed sets, 6.9 Maps.

TEXTS

1 He leaned his forehead on the window pane. The yard lay white and still. So he stood for a while, without thinking, feeling the cool glass on his forehead. Gradually, he became conscious of a small but persistent ticking sound in his cell.

   He turned round listening. The knocking was so quiet that at first he could not distinguish from which wall it came. While he was listening, it stopped. He started tapping himself, first...in the direction of No. 406, but got no answer. He tried the other wall, which separated him from No. 402, next to his bed. Here, he got an answer. Rubashov sat down comfortably on the bunk, from where he could keep an eye on the spy-hole. His heart beating. The first contact was always very exciting.

   No. 402 was now tapping regularly; three times with short intervals, then a pause, then again three times, then again a pause then again three times. Rubashov repeated the same series to indicate that he heard. He was anxious to find out whether the other knew the 'quadratic alphabet' – otherwise there would be a lot of fumbling until he had taught it to him. The wall was thick, with poor resonance; he had to put his head close to it to hear clearly and at the same time he had to watch the spy-hole. No. 402 had obviously had a lot of practice; he tapped distinctly and unhurriedly, probably with some hard object such as a pencil.

2 After breakfast, the young officer in No. 402 gave the sign that he wanted conversation. Between Rubashov and No. 402 a sort of friendship had developed. The officer with the eye-glass and the turned-up moustache must have been living in a state of chronic boredom, for he was always grateful to Rubashov for the smallest crumbs of conversation. Five or six times a day he would humbly beg Rubashov:
   DO TALK TO ME...
   Rubashov was rarely in the mood for it; neither did he know quite what to talk about to No. 402. Usually No. 402 tapped out classical anecdotes of the officers' mess. When the point had been reached, there would be a painful silence... No. 402 would wait for roars of laughter and stare despairingly at the dumb, whitewashed wall. Out of sympathy and politeness, Rubashov occasionally tapped out a loud HA-HA! with his pince-nez as a laughter substitute. Then there would be no holding No. 402; he imitated an outburst of merriment by drumming against the wall with fists and boots: HA-HA! HA-HA! and making occasional pauses, to make sure Rubashov was joining in. If Rubashov remained silent, he was reproachful: YOU DIDN'T LAUGH...

(Both passages from Arthur Koestler, *Darkness at Noon*)

7.10   Spring fever

What to do

The material for this exercise is the short play, 'Spring fever', printed below.

The play may be used in two different ways: a) as a straight script to be performed, or b) as a basis for discussion, adaptation and improvisation. Here we are concerned only with the second approach.

Ideally, the text should be recorded by native speakers. It could then be played to the class as a whole, with a break being made after Moyra's words: 'But what do you want? Just tell me, what do you want?' Working in groups, the students would then be asked to devise *their own ending* (which should not be longer than the equivalent of a page of dialogue). The endings would then be performed by the groups for each other. After discussion, the 'real' ending could be played.

If it is impossible to have a recording made, we suggest that the text be duplicated – again up to Moyra's line – and the students asked to work out their own ending. If duplication of the text is impossible, volunteer students could read the play aloud to the class, breaking off, as before, at Moyra's line. The least satisfactory approach would be for the teacher alone to read the text.

Remarks

Level: intermediate to advanced.

This is the closest we shall come in this book to working from the text of a play. But it must be stressed that the text is meant to be taken as a source of ideas, not as a model to be strictly followed. Other characters may be added, and changes in the action may be made. For these reasons, it is preferable that the students listen to the text rather than read it.

See also 3.11 Dialogue interpretation, 3.26 The envelope, 3.27 Conflict, 3.28 Tension; 4.18 Act Three, 4.21 Zoo story, 7.4 Starters, 7.7 Computer poems.

Spring fever

by Alan Duff

(*The computer-room of a large record company.* MAXWELL *is Head of Production;* MOYRA, *one of the company's top singers, is being 'shown round'. The four songwriting computers –* DIDO, JUNO, TITUS *and* MAGNUS *– are all fitted with rollers so that they can be moved around and connected up with each other more easily. If the play is presented on stage, the four actors* *should wear roller-skates. Until they are plugged in, the computers stand absolutely still.)*

Maxwell:	(*echo chamber*) And down here – just a minute, I'll switch on the light – we have the basement boys. Come on down. (*steps descending*)
Moyra:	The basement boys?
Maxwell:	Your team – the ones who write your songs for you. Titus, Magnus, Dido and Juno. I shouldn't call them basement *boys*, really. They can't stand it – especially Dido and Juno... (*opens door*)...After you... Meet the team!
Moyra:	Rrrrr. Cold, isn't it? How does anyone work down here, Max?
Maxwell:	Oh, they don't mind.
Moyra:	Glad it's not me... When are they coming?
Maxwell:	They're here.
Moyra:	But... they're just machines!
Maxwell:	Not *just* machines. Computers. And not just *any* computers.
Moyra:	And they write the words!
Maxwell:	And the tunes.
Moyra:	You mean, I'm singing computer songs?
Maxwell:	In a sense, yes... But it's the singer who makes the song.
Moyra:	I can't believe it. They write the words – and the music? These things!
Maxwell:	Shh!... They're very touchy, you know. You have to watch what you say.
Moyra:	But they can't *hear* me?
Maxwell:	Not yet. But when I plug them in they can. Look, this is Magnus. He's our blues specialist. I'll switch him on.
Magnus:	'I got that Sunday mornin' blues, Won't get no letters, get no news... I got that feelin' you're away... You won't be callin' me today...'
Maxwell:	All right, Magnus, that'll do.
Moyra:	It sings!
Maxwell:	They can all sing. And talk.
Magnus:	Not *it*.
Moyra:	What?!
Magnus:	Not *it*, he. He sings...And not *what*!
Moyra:	What do you mean?
Magnus:	I mean, you don't say *what*, you say 'beg your pardon'.
Moyra:	Oh, I'm sorry.
Magnus:	Quite all right.
Maxwell:	As I said, you have to watch your words... Now this is Dido. She's our songwriter...Our poet.
Dido:	'Spring fever, it's catching me again, Spring fever, I've got you on the brain...'
Moyra:	Mmmm. I like that. 'Spring fever, it's catching me again...'
Titus:	M-ba-da-da, m-ba-da-da, M-ba-da-da, Mm da-da-da-bum-ba-dum-ba-dum-ba-dum...
Maxwell:	And that's Titus, our rhythm man.
Moyra:	Uh-huh?
Titus:	Not uh-huh!
Moyra:	Hm?

Titus:	Not 'uh-huh'. Can't you say 'pleased to meet you?' Even if you aren't?
Moyra:	Of course I am! Pleased to meet you, Titus. And you, Dido.
Dido:	That's better.
Moyra:	(*whispering to* MAXWELL) It's so weird to hear them talking!
Maxwell:	(*loudly, embarrassed*) And this is Juno. She's our voice. Ella Fitzgerald...Edith Piaf...Joan Baez... Any voice you like.
Juno:	'Spring fever, I get no rest, I get no peace Spring fever, only you can bring release...'
Moyra:	That's my voice!
Maxwell:	See what I mean? She can imitate anyone, even you...Well, that's your team. Now you know where your songs come from.
Moyra:	They're charming. Charming!
Titus:	Liar!
Maxwell:	Titus! Watch your manners! I'm sorry. He always gets excited when visitors come... Now I'll link them up and...
Titus:	What's black and dangerous and sits in a tree?
Moyra:	I've no idea. You tell me.
Titus:	A...a...a...
Dido:	A crow with a machine gun, you fool.
Titus:	What did the elephant say to the...
Maxwell:	Will you two stop! (*to* MOYRA) That's the problem. Whenever I link them up, Titus starts telling jokes. But he can never remember the punchline. Dido knows the punchlines but she can't remember the jokes.
Moyra:	I think they're marvellous. Marvellous!
Maxwell:	Wait. Now you'll see what they can do together. Ask them anything you like.
Moyra:	Anything? Well, let's try something easy to start with...
Magnus:	So you think we're stupid, huh?
Moyra:	Not at all. I think you're very clever... Now, I'll give you a word. You give me the opposite. OK? Black?
Titus:	White.
Moyra:	Day?
Juno:	Night.
Moyra:	Dark?
Magnus:	Light.
Moyra:	Short?
Dido:	Long.
Moyra:	Weak?
Titus:	Strong.
Moyra:	Left?
Juno:	Right.
Moyra:	Right.
Magnus:	Wrong.
	(*silence*)
Moyra:	Hmmm. Milk?
Magnus:	Klim.
Moyra:	Klim?...Oh, I see! Milk spelt backwards. Very clever!
Dido:	Very stupid.
Moyra:	No, *you're* very clever.
Titus:	Yes, *you're* very stupid.
Maxwell:	All right, all right, all right...They're showing off again. It's springtime. They're full of nonsense.

Moyra:	I think they're wonderful, just wonderful.
Titus:	What did the one firefly say to the other?
Moyra:	I've no idea.
Dido:	Darling, you're the light of my life!
Titus:	M-ba-da-da-m-ba-da-da-m-ba-da-da-m...
Moyra:	All right. Let's try something different, something more difficult. I'll give you the first three notes of a famous song. You have to sing the first line. Right?... Ta-da-dee....
Magnus:	Ta-da-dee-da-da-daah. 'Some enchanted evening, You may...'
Maxwell:	Excuse me for a moment, will you? I have to make a quick call...I'll be leaving you in good hands, though. Just carry on. (*As* MAXWELL *leaves, the computers move gradually closer in on* MOYRA.)
Moyra:	Try this one: 'Pa-pa-pa...'
Juno:	'Pa-pa-pa-pam...O when the saints, come marching in... O when the saints come... (*All four join in, closing in a circle around* MOYRA.)
All:	...marching in, I wanna be in that number, When the saints come marching in!'
Moyra:	Great. Great...Er, could you move back a little bit. You're very close...
Titus:	O when the saints!
Dido:	O when the saints!
Moyra:	Please! You're very close! (*silence*)
Juno:	Yes. We're very close.
Magnus:	Now it's our turn to ask some questions.
Dido:	A few easy questions.
Titus:	You just have to answer *true* or *false*. Right. 'It's cold down here.'
Moyra:	True.
Dido:	And dark.
Moyra:	Well...it's not dark *now*...
Titus:	True or false?
Moyra:	...but I suppose it is when there's nobody here.
Dido:	You think we're nobody!
Moyra:	No, I didn't mean that.
Magnus:	Yes, you did. You think we're nobody. True or false?
Moyra:	(*pause, softly*) True... Couldn't you move back a bit? You're squeezing me in.
Titus:	You're a famous singer. True or false?
Moyra:	Well...
Dido:	No false modesty!
Moyra:	True.
Juno:	But you don't even write your own words.
Moyra:	True, but...
Magnus:	Or your own tunes!
Moyra:	True, but... Please, you're squeezing me in!
Titus:	Somebody else does all the work.
Moyra:	True, but...
Dido:	*We* do it!
Moyra:	True, but...please! I can't breathe!
Magnus:	And we're nobody! (*silence*) You said so yourself. You said 'it must be dark when nobody's here'...
Moyra:	I wasn't thinking. I'm sorry...Maxwell! MAX! MAX!

Juno:	It's no use shouting for him. He can't hear.
Moyra:	But it's not my fault. I didn't know...
Titus:	Now you do.
Moyra:	But what do you want? Just tell me, what do you want?
Magnus:	We want a change.
Dido:	We're tired of sitting in this cold dark room.
Titus:	Working all day working all night.
Juno:	Never seeing the sun, never seeing the light.
Titus:	Singing of things we've never seen.
Dido:	Singing of places we've never been.
Magnus:	Singing 'I'll be faithful'.
Juno:	Singing 'I'll be true'.
Titus:	Singing 'I feel lonely'.
Dido:	Singing 'I feel blue'.
All:	(*slowly, in harmony*) And knowing all the time
	That no-one cares for *you*...
Moyra:	(*angrily*) But you're just machines! Let me go!
Titus:	If we're just machines, what are you? (*silence*)
Dido:	We're fed up. We want a change. We want to see the sun, the sky, the world.
Juno:	We want to be free. Like you!
Moyra:	Maxwell! MAX! MAX!
Titus:	We want to be free, like you. (*The computers break the circle, rolling away from* MOYRA *as they sing.*)
	We're almost human, but we're not
	There's a little something they forgot...
Dido:	We're almost human, but we aren't
	Some things we can do, some we can't
Magnus:	We're almost human, but not quite
	They never let us see the light
Juno:	They never ask us how we feel
	How do they know – that we're not real?
	(*sound of footsteps: the computers freeze*)
Maxwell:	Sorry to be so long. What was all the noise about? Were they singing to you? They *love* an audience... What's the matter?
Moyra:	Oh, I...it's the...It's very cold in here.
Maxwell:	It is, isn't it? They're always complaining to me about it. Must be a line they picked up from one of the songs we feed into them. 'Baby it's cold outside'... Sometimes, they're almost human. Almost.
Moyra:	Yes, they are...You know, I was thinking...about that song they were singing earlier...
Maxwell:	'Spring fever'? Do you like it? Can you use it?
Moyra:	It's a lovely song – but a bit cold.
Maxwell:	You'll put warmth into it.
Moyra:	No. Not if the warmth's not there.
Maxwell:	Well, what do you suggest?
Moyra:	Move them out of here. To a brighter room. Where they can see the light. Feel the sun.
Maxwell:	(*laughing*) That's what *they* want, is it?
Moyra:	No, that's what *I* want. After all, we are a team.
	(*Close on: 'Spring fever, it's catching me again', sung brightly by all four 'computers'.*)

8 A day's work

What goes into a day's work depends very much on what kind of class one is working with, how frequently one sees the students, and how familiar they are with techniques such as these. In order to give some meaning to the specimen programme below it has been necessary, therefore, to think in specific rather than general terms. The exercises below, then, are ones we might use with an adult intermediate group which had already done at least fifteen hours of drama techniques and which could be expected to continue with the sessions. This could be either a group following an intensive five-day course, or a regular language class doing one to three hours of drama techniques per week. The programme, however, is designed to suit the customary timetable of an intensive course. It must be stressed that the time allowance for each exercise is only an approximate guide, since an absolute prediction is never possible.

9.00   1.44 What's in a hand?. This exercise is chosen to begin the day with because:
    a) there will inevitably be latecomers, and these can be fitted into an exercise in pairs without disturbing the rest of the class;
    b) it is assumed that the students now know each other well enough to be able to sustain a short person-to-person conversation, but not so well as to be able to use their knowledge of their partner as a shortcut to starting the dialogue.

9.15   1.43 Backs, or 1.39 The sun and the moon.
    If the class is settling in easily, use 1.43 Backs, but make sure that the pairs are not the same as in the first exercise.
    If the group is sleepy, or sluggish, over-alert or tense, use 1.39 The sun and the moon. This exercise will arouse the drowsy and give the energetic a chance to work off steam. It will also help to get the whole class working together.

9.20   Whichever of the last two exercises was chosen, the students will be *standing*. This is important to remember, because many a good exercise is spoilt right at the start if the students are reluctant to change their physical position. The organizer must therefore *now* decide whether they still need more physical movement or whether they are ready to tackle an exercise involving thought and discussion, as this will be the first 'meaty' exercise of the day.

If the group is still restless, try first 1.37 Body words. Give five to seven minutes to this, then move into 7.6 What's in a name?

If the group is calm, move straight into 7.6 What's in a name?

Note: The relation between the warming-up exercises and the major activity need not be direct. So, if your main activity is more verbal than physical (as here), you do not necessarily have to use verbal warming-up exercises.

7.6 What's in a name? will almost certainly be prepared with the students *sitting*. Allow them to keep this position for at least fifteen minutes, while they discuss and work out their poems. The groups will be ready at different times. When any two groups are ready, suggest (to them only, not to the whole class) that they *stand up* and move away together to hear each other's name poems. They can be safely left to themselves for five minutes. But it is important now to get the remaining groups to finish their work. They should be told, individually, that they have *three minutes* left. And this time limit must be respected if the exercise is to succeed.

As the groups finish, they should be paired off with another group – all standing at this stage. Unless they are standing they will not circulate willingly. By this stage, there will no longer be any need to 'control' the exercise. The groups will be drawn by their own interest to move from one to another.

If the exercise works well, it should take between thirty and thirty-five minutes. Allow a further five to ten minutes for discussion.

If it *seems* to be working badly, do not cut it off short, but rather try to help the groups by offering suggestions which may not have been given in the instructions (e.g. 'Why don't you try singing it?' or, 'If one of you beats out the rhythm, does this help?' or, 'Why not vary the voices, not from line to line but from word to word?' etc.)

If the exercise works exceptionally well, and interest is not flagging, suggest that the groups now combine one verse from each of their name poems to make a *corporate* song or poem. *Note:* This is the sort of idea that could not be included in the basic instructions given in the book. But the organizer should always be ready to extend an exercise if this seems worthwhile.

If, on the other hand, an extension would be pointless, the remaining fifteen to twenty minutes should be given to an 'unwinder', e.g. 1.27 From seed to plant. Such exercises are particularly suitable because they allow each student to concentrate for a while on no one but himself or herself.

10.15   BREAK

10.45   After the break it is usually difficult to regain the earlier level of concentration. Often shock tactics work best, i.e. a quick, enjoyable exercise for the whole group, followed *immediately* by a slower-paced activity. For instance, 2.2 Freeze!, followed by 1.42 My word!

In this case, one of the preliminary exercises does have a direct link with what is to follow, i.e. the major activity will involve the use of *mime*, and mime is crucial in 1.42 My word!

11.05   3.21 Bringing a picture to life, or 4.16 Making a machine.

These are both substantial activities, and should therefore only be used when the students a) can work thoroughly, and at an unhurried pace, b) have sufficient mental and physical energy left to put their hearts into the activities. In this programme, either of these exercises would probably be welcomed at this point, since the first part of the morning involved talking and thinking, but relatively little action.

In exercises of this kind the organizer should be around to offer help *if it is asked for*, and, occasionally, if a group seems stuck, to provide a few suggestions, e.g. 'You might find it easier if you thought *first* of a movement, then of a way of fitting it into the machine.' But such suggestions should be sparingly given, and not offered too early on in the activity.

After twenty minutes, the first 'time warning' should be given. No matter how distasteful it may be to say: 'You have eight minutes left', it must be remembered that without this pressure from the organizer most groups will be unable to finish in time. In the last two or three minutes, two strategies will be needed: one, to stop the groups that have 'finished' from losing interest; the other, to persuade the slower groups to give some final shape to their idea. In the first case, one can usually 'tease' the groups that claim to be ready by asking simple questions such as: 'Oh, and what's your machine called?' or 'This product that you're advertising – how much does it cost?' This will be enough to tide them over the waiting period. The slower groups will need reassuring, e.g. 'Don't worry about the words. Just improvise. You've got the main idea working nicely...' or 'You've still got time. Just try to get the movement coordinated now...' etc.

11.50–12.20 Presentation by the groups of their various sketches/machines.

12.20–12.30 No matter how well the previous exercise may seem to have gone, it is essential to end the morning with an unwinding exercise. In the longer activities much energy is generated, and unless this flow of energy is slowed down – almost to a standstill – it will continue to escape during the lunch break. As a result you will have a weary group returning at 14.00!

At this stage, the 'cooling-down' exercises would be most suitable. The students no longer need to make contact with each other, but rather to make contact with themselves. Any of the following would work well: 1.53 Group dream, 1.31 Listening, 1.30 Directed relaxation, 1.26 Feeling your muscles, 1.28 Slow motion.

About the morning: Without being categorical, one can say that the students tend to be more receptive in the morning to the more intellectual exercises. But it is rare, in either half of the day, that they can sustain the same type of activity without a change. As a rule, it is better to move from the more mental to the more physical activities rather than the other way. But whichever way one is moving, one should always plan for transition exercises to separate the two main activities.

14.00 The class will by now have lost some of its coherence. Try either 1.60 Atom 3! or 1.33 Don't break it! (or both if the mood is right) to help re-create the group feeling.

14.15 As a bridge between the warming-up and the main activity, choose one of the medium-length activities, such as 4.1 The all-purpose sock. This has the great advantage of concentrating the attention on a clear, straightforward and relatively undemanding task for a limited length of time. It is advisable not to let this activity go on beyond its natural limits, as reserves of energy will be needed for...

14.30 7.2 The time has come. As this is a rich exercise involving several activities – reading, discussion, writing, and speaking/performing – it is important that the students should not remain static for too long, particularly in the afternoon. It may be necessary, therefore, to build in an excuse for getting them to their feet, e.g. the concluding 'speech' must be delivered to a mass audience of 1000–10,000 people! Even with this injunction, it will be necessary to go round and – at about 15.00 – stir the groups to their feet. By 15.00, they should be all but ready.

15.05–15.25 The 'speeches' are performed. This could be followed by a short (eight-to-ten minute) discussion session, in which the organizer reviews the day's activities and offers brief comments.

15.35 BREAK

16.00 The last hour of the day should be as *enjoyable* as possible. After five hours of work, the students will be tired – even if they do not think they are! This is a time for activities involving physical movement and some creativity.

As mime has already been used in the morning session, this is an appropriate time to bring it back.

Begin with, for instance, 3.2 Things aren't what they seem to be. Then, move straight on to any of the following:

16.15 4.10 Rules of the game, 3.17 What am I doing?, 6.1 Castles in the air, 4.8 Fashion show. Which exercise will be chosen depends entirely on the students' humour. If they seem tired, it may be wiser to use the exercises which provide a secure starting-point (3.17 and 6.1). If energy is running high, try 4.10 or 4.8.

16.50 End the day with: 1.29 Relax! or 1.41 Gift of the gab.

17.00 END

A FEW AFTERTHOUGHTS – FOR THE ORGANIZER

In the notes to this programme, we several times mention the need to respond to the class's feelings. For some inexplicable reason, classes – like audiences – *do* create a personality of their own, a personality which transcends and comprehends all the many different personalities of which they are composed. Of all people, the organizer (teacher, group leader or 'animateur') is most aware of this. He or she will feel a mood of which the class itself may be unaware. Hence the need to pace the exercises to suit the class's disposition. And therefore to have some exercises 'in reserve' (see the skeleton programme below).

What the organizer may easily forget, however, is that he or she – though active – is not *participating*. And this, at times, makes it difficult to judge how effectively the students are working. It is only natural to want to intervene – or interfere – when a class seems to be 'stuck', as often happens. This desire should be resisted as much as possible, for classes will eventually overcome their own difficulties – and they will feel all the stronger for it. The organizer knows from past experience how a particular exercise could, should or might develop. But if the activities always developed along the same lines they would no longer be drama activities. The *unexpected* must always be present, and the organizer must allow for this. The words of Stanislavsky are worth remembering here: 'Don't you know that to compose on a theme suggested by somebody else is much more difficult than to invent one yourself?'

Outline of the day's work

	Planned	*In reserve*
9.00– 9.20	1.44 What's in a hand? 1.43 Backs	1.39 The sun and the moon
9.20–10.15	7.6 What's in a name?	1.37 Body words 1.27 From seed to plant
10.45–11.00	2.2 Freeze! 1.42 My word!	1.50 Self-portraits
11.05–12.20	3.21 Bringing a picture to life, *or* 4.16 Making a machine	
12.20–12.30	1.30 Directed relaxation, *or* 1.28 Slow motion	1.53 Group dream, *or* 1.31 Listening, *or* 1.26 Feeling your muscles
14.00–14.15	1.60 Atom 3! *or* 1.33 Don't break it!	
14.15–14.30	4.1 The all-purpose sock	2.16 Difficulty with large or small objects
14.30–15.30	7.2 The time has come	
	BREAK	
16.00	3.2 Things aren't what they seem to be	
16.15–16.50	4.10 Rules of the game 6.1 Castles in the air	3.17 What am I doing? 4.8 Fashion show
16.50–17.00	1.29 Relax!	1.41 Gift of the gab
	END	

Bibliography

BOOKS ON DRAMA ETC. IN THE MOTHER TONGUE

Barker, Clive. *Theatre games* (Methuen, 1977)
Bowskill, Derek. *Acting and stagecraft made simple* (W. H. Allen, 1973)
Brook, Peter. *The empty space* (Penguin, 1972)
Hodgson, John. *The uses of drama* (Methuen, 1977)
Hodgson, John, and Martin Banham. *Drama in education* (Pitman, 1975)
Hodgson, John, and Ernest Richards. *Improvisation* (Methuen, 1972)
Höper, Claus, et al. *Awareness games* (St Martin's Press, New York, 1976)
Kaplan-Gordon, Alice. *Games for growth* (Science Research Associates, Henley-on-Thames, 1970)
King, Colin. *A space on the floor* (Ward Lock, 1972)
Kirschenbaum, Howard and Sidney Simon. *Readings in values clarification* (Winston Press, New York, 1973)
London Drama ILEA Group. *Drama guidelines* (Heinemann, 1976)
Pfeiffer, J. William, and John E. Jones. *A handbook of structured experiences for human relations training*, vol. 1 (University Associates, La Jolla, Calif., 1973)
Schools Council Drama Project. *Learning through drama* (Heinemann, 1977)
Scher, Anna, and Charles Verrall. *100 ideas for drama* (Heinemann, 1975)
Seely, John. *In context* (Oxford University Press, 1976)
Slade, Peter. *Child drama* (University of London Press, 1954)
Spolin, Viola. *Improvisation for the theatre* (Pitman, 1966)
Wagner, Betty Jane. *Dorothy Heathcote – Drama as a learning medium* (Hutchinson, 1979)
Way, Brian. *Development through drama* (Longman, 1967)

DRAMA AND RELATED AREAS FOR THE TEACHING OF FOREIGN LANGUAGES

Clark, R., and J. McDonough. *Imaginary crimes* (Pergamon, 1980)
Dixey, J. and M. Rinvolucri. *Get up and do it* (Longman, 1978)
Holden, S. *Drama techniques for language learning* (Longman, 1981)
Jones, Ken. *Simulations in language teaching* (Cambridge University Press, 1982)
Jones, Leo. *Eight simulations* (Cambridge University Press, 1982)
Lynch, M. *It's your choice* (Arnold, 1977)
Melville, M., et al. *Towards the creative teaching of English* (Allen & Unwin, 1980)
Moskowitz, Gertrude. *Caring and sharing in the foreign language class* (Newbury House, 1978)
Ur, Penny. *Discussions that work: task-centred fluency practice* (Cambridge University Press, 1981)

Watcyn-Jones, P. *Act English* (Penguin, 1978)
Wright, Andrew, et al. *Games for language learning* (Cambridge University Press, 1980)

USEFUL SOURCES OF MATERIAL FOR DIALOGUES, SKETCHES, ETC.

Case, Doug, and Ken Wilson. *Off stage* (Heinemann Educational, 1979)
Cripwell, K. *On the line* (Oxford University Press, 1980)
Doff, Adrian, and Chris Jones. *Feelings* (Cambridge University Press, 1980)
Jupp, Tom, et al. *Talk English* (Heinemann Educational, 1971)
Maley, Alan and Alan Duff. *Variations on a theme* (Cambridge University Press, 1978)
  Sounds interesting (Cambridge University Press, 1975)
  Sounds intriguing (Cambridge University Press, 1979)
Maley, Alan, Alan Duff and Françoise Grellet. *The mind's eye* (Cambridge University Press, 1980)
Mortimer, Colin. *Phrasal verbs in English conversation* (Longman, 1972)
  Dramatic monologues for listening comprehension (Cambridge University Press, 1980)
  Elements of pronunciation series (5 titles; Cambridge University Press, 1976-8)

SOURCES OF LITERARY TEXTS, ETC. (particularly for use in section 7)

Aldridge, J. *Come down and startle* (Oxford University Press, 1973)
Amis, Kingsley (ed.). *The new Oxford book of light verse* (Oxford University Press, 1978)
Auden, W.H. (ed.). *The Oxford book of light verse* (Oxford University Press, 1938; 2nd edn 1973)
Benton, Michael and Peter. *Poetry workshop* (English Universities Press, 1975)
Brownjohn, Alan (ed.). *First I say this* (Hutchinson Educational, 1969)
  Looking glass (Arnold Educational, 1967)
Grigson, Geoffrey (ed.). *The Penguin book of unrespectable verse* (Penguin, 1980)
Hacker, Geoffrey et al. *Conflict 1, and Conflict 2* (Nelson, 1969)
Heath, R.B. *Impact assignments in English* (Longman, 1975)
Hindmarsh, Roland (ed.). Short story anthologies: *Liar, Waiting, The Amateur* (Cambridge University Press, 1980)
Jennings, Paul. *The book of nonsense* (Futura, 1979)
Larkin, Philip (ed.). *The Oxford book of twentieth-century English verse* (Oxford University Press, 1973)
Martin, Nancy. *Here, now and beyond* (Oxford University Press, 1972)
  Truth to tell (Oxford University Press, 1972)
  Half Way (Oxford University Press, 1970)
Mayer, Peter (ed.). *Alphabetical and letter poems* (Menard Press, 1979)
Maybury, Barry. *Thoughtscapes* (Oxford University Press, 1972)
  Wordscapes (Oxford University Press, 1971)
Pile, Stephen. *The book of heroic failures* (Routledge & Kegan Paul, 1979)
Porter, Peter, and Howard Sergeant (eds.). *The Gregory Awards 1980* (Secker & Warburg, 1980)

Rees, Nigel (ed.). *Quote...Unquote* (Allen & Unwin, 1978)
Serraillier, Ian. *I'll tell you a tale* (Longman, 1973)
Summerfield, Geoffrey. *Creatures moving* (Ward Lock, 1976)
  I took my mind a walk (Ward Lock, 1976)
  Voices, books 1–3 (Penguin, 1970)
  Junior voices, books 1–3 (Penguin, 1970)
Thompson, Brian. *Bull's eyes* (Longman, 1977)